John Ogden

CW01638490

THE RAGGED TROUSERED AIRMAN

The Ragged Trousered AIRMAN

Jack Davidson

UNITED WRITERS
Cornwall

UNITED WRITERS PUBLICATIONS LTD
Ailsa, Castle Gate, Penzance, Cornwall.

All Rights Reserved. No part of this publication may be reproduced, stored in a retrieval system, or transmitted, in any form or by any means, electronic, mechanical, photocopying, recording or otherwise, without the prior permission of the Copyright owner.

British Library Cataloguing in Publication Data:
A catalogue record for this book is
available from the British Library.

ISBN 9781852001452

Copyright © 2010 Jack Davidson

Printed in Great Britain by
United Writers Publications Ltd
Cornwall.

To my old comrades in arms:

Harry Birkenhead – 1st driver
Frank Routledge – 2nd driver
Harry Clark – wireless opp.
Yoddy Mills – wireless opp.
Archie Osborne – observer
Frank Smith – observer

Preface

Having seen many films and read quite a few books about the Second World War, I found that they all seem to have one thing in common; they all had heroes who were usually officers.

In my service career I didn't meet many officers except when I was on pay parade or when on a charge for misbehaving.

I am not implying there weren't any heroes, for if that had been the case we wouldn't have won the war.

What I am saying is that I never met one.

This is a true story about a lad who was brought up in a lower working class area, joined the RAF when he was eighteen on the 19th of July 1940, travelled a lot of the world, and saw happy and sad times. My main aim, along with the other ninety-five per cent of service men, was to survive without bothering too much about King and Country.

Contents

1
Starting Work

Easter couldn't come soon enough that year. It was 1936 and I left school on a Friday. After listening to my elders saying 'What you need these days, lad, is a trade,' I started to look at the situations vacant in the *Telegraph and Argus*. At first I fancied being a joiner, until, on about the third night, there was a vacancy that took my fancy which read: 'Painter and decorator apprentice wanted. Apply: Ralph Young, 17 Thorn Lane, Haworth Road.' I had no idea where Haworth Road was, except that it went from somewhere in Heaton to Haworth. The next night, after my tea, off I went to find it. I didn't tell my parents or anyone else, for the simple reason that if I failed to get the job there would be no one to taunt or mock me. I didn't know what an inferiority complex was at the time but I certainly had one. It was the same four years later when I went to join the RAF. I didn't tell anyone then, but there wasn't any fear of me not getting that one.

I caught the tram from Bradford to Allerton. I had worked out that if I went to Allerton and walked down to Sandy Lane I would be forced to cross Haworth Road at some point. Which I did, and when I got there I asked a local where Thorn Lane was. It was an Irish mile away so it was late when I arrived. There was another youth leaving when I got to No 17. He looked a smart lad in his best suit and with his shoes polished, so it crossed my mind that I hadn't a chance. So much so, I nearly turned round and went home. Unfortunately, Mrs Young had seen me coming up the garden path and was at the back door to ask me in. Mr Young was in the front room where he was doing his interviewing.

What struck me most was the decorating. I had never seen anything like it, not even on films. The house was a detached bungalow so it didn't have a staircase. The hall walls were panels of leather but not real leather, because they were painted in such a way that it was hard to tell. The doors had four panels, the top panel was about two feet square and the remainder were beautifully grained, imitating wood with paint, in a dark English oak. The top panel was made to look like vellum and in each panel was a verse from the *Rubaiyat of Omar Khayyam* in illuminated lettering. I got to know those verses well and my favourite was:

'The Moving Finger writes; and, having writ,
Moves on: nor all thy Piety nor Wit
Shall lure it back to cancel half a line,
Nor all thy tears wash out a Word of it.'

The front room also had me fascinated. The two main walls were covered with murals of trees, birds and small animals. The chimney breast was a plain neutral colour with two butterflies, painted in three dimensions, so much so that they looked to be flying out at you off the wall.

The first thing Mr Young asked me was why I wanted to be a decorator. I told him drawing and painting was the only thing I had been good at in school. I declined from mentioning the rugby because even though he was a big man he had not got the look of a rugby type. He had more the look of Rasputin the mad monk. After a few more questions he informed me the wage would be 10/- (50p) a week and that if I didn't get a postcard by Monday I hadn't got the job. No sign of a postcard on Monday, so that was that, or so I thought.

After tea on Monday evening there was a loud knock on the front door. My mother answered the door and there he was, all six foot and a bit. My mother got a bit of a shock as she immediately took him for a detective looking for me or my brother. Not that I had been a bad lad up to then. He explained who he was and came in. He had come to see if I had any of my paintings to show him. Whether it was that he didn't believe my tale about it being the only thing I was good at or if he wanted to see if I really had any talent I am not sure, but he must have been impressed as he asked me when I could start. I soon found out that art was the only thing he thought about. He didn't drink, smoke, swear, believe in god or siring children, much to his wife's regret.

The following Monday I was up bright and early and off to learn a trade in my short white coat and apron. The first lesson was to speak when you were spoken to and that went for both the customers and the men. The next lesson was how to fold my apron and roll it up so that it fitted neatly into my coat pocket. The third lesson was how to handle the handcart. You may think that would be easy but when loading up, which I did nearly every morning, I had to make sure that it was properly balanced. When pushing it I had to keep it pushed into the kerb to let cars go past, which was impossible when going up steep hills as I had to zigzag from one side of the road to another, like sailing a yacht against the wind. I had to put my right hand out and make for the centre of the road when turning right. That came in handy for when I got my first bicycle. The miles I did with that cart was nobody's business. The worst part of it was that Mr Y had a car and trailer, but for 10/- a week it was cheaper to use me as a little donkey.

The first job I went on was with the boss – a bedroom; to strip and paper the walls and distemper the ceiling. We covered the furniture with dustsheets and got cracking. At lunchtime I took our pots with the mashing in them to the lady of the house and she mashed our tea. A mashing was sugar put on to a piece of newspaper followed by a dollop of condensed milk, the tea was then put on top of the milk and wrapped up scientifically in the newspaper, hoping the tea and sugar would prevent the milk from sticking to the paper.

Ralph sat on the bed to eat his sandwiches. I eyed a low bit of the dressing table which had the sheet on it, I sat myself down there to partake of my corned beef sandwiches. There was a crash; I had sat on a glass shelf! Although Ralph didn't swear he had other words to express his feelings like 'As sure as God made little apples' and 'God strike one'. That was after my first half day. He told me if there was no improvement in my antics by Friday it was down the road. There were times when I wished it had happened during the next three and a half years. Besides him giving me a thorough training in the trade and improving my artistic talents, he never hit me. Not like the other three men that worked for him, they gave me a clout around the earhole on most days. I never hit them back, although as I had been playing rugby a couple of years I would have been quite capable of doing so. It wasn't the thing to strike your elders.

The days, the months and the years went by like they do. At night, in the winter, I went to the Bradford College of Arts and Crafts, studying for the City and Guilds exam. Some of my pals went on day release. Mr Young wouldn't let me go as he said he couldn't afford to let me have the time off.

It didn't take much working out why he couldn't afford to give me the time off, for when I was seventeen I was paperhanging, graining and sign writing, and he was charging the customers improver's rate of 1/6d (7½p) an hour and paying me 17/6d a week. You don't have to be a mastermind in maths to work that one out.

Sometimes in the winter, when there was no work locally, we would go to Colne or Nelson in Lancashire to do jobs, as that was where Mr Young was brought up. When he didn't take me with him I was left at the workshop to paint and re-letter the ladders, trestles and handcart, together with other jobs like turning the garden over when it wasn't frozen and cleaning the windows, etc.

Mrs Young was a kind woman. When her husband went on these trips she would ask me to have my tea and sandwiches sat in front of the fire in the kitchen and give me magazines called the *Passing Show* to read.

One such day, when I had finished my lunch and was warming up to go back into the workshop, she said she was going to have a bath. As I was getting up to go back into the workshop I heard her calling 'Jack.' I went to the bathroom door and what she wanted was a towel from the airing cupboard in the kitchen. At the time, being a naïve youth, it never crossed my mind that she wanted anything but the towel.

Taking the towel I knocked on the bathroom door and went in. I had never seen a naked woman before and I got a funny feeling in my lower regions.

Many a time afterwards, when I looked back on this incident, I discovered what Adam must have felt like when he first set his eyes on the forbidden fruit.

My eighteenth birthday came and I was looking forward to getting a shilling an hour as an improver, but was disappointed as all I received in my pay packet on the Friday was a pound.

On the Saturday morning I plucked up courage and told Mr Young I was leaving him if he didn't pay more. He tried to frighten me by saying that if there was no work in the winter he would lay me off and I would have no wage at all.

As quick as a flash I calculated that I could be laid off for six months and still be better off, so I stuck to my guns and he relented; it caused him to sulk for a few days. He was one of the best sulkers I have ever met; and as for being out of work, there was a decorating firm down Toller Lane owned by a man called Frank Needham, and every time he saw me behind the handcart he offered me a job and added, 'You wouldn't be pushing that thing if you worked for me.' However, I don't think I would have learned my trade with him as well as I had with Mr Young.

It was the spring of 1940, the war was in full swing and things weren't looking so good. We, the British, had been kicked out of France at Dunkirk and it looked as if the Germans were going to invade England at any minute. What the Germans didn't know was that Jack was going to join up; neither did Jack at the time.

2
Joining Up

On Saturday afternoons in summer my pal Austin and I usually went into town and had a walk round the market. There was nothing much else to do, as the rugby season had finished and to my mind watching cricket was like waiting for Christmas.

On this particular afternoon, which was as I remember a dull, drizzly day like we get sometimes in July, there was a lull in our conversation and all of a sudden Austin said, 'Shall we join the Navy?' I remember vividly where we were at the time; passing the Prince's Theatre at the bottom of Horton Lane which was demolished a long time ago. Where it stood is now the site of the National Media Museum.

His suggestion stopped me in my tracks. I just stood there looking at a poster proclaiming that the Hanson Players were appearing in 'Wuthering Heights' the following week.

Horrible thoughts went through my mind; I was imagining myself out on the cold North Sea swabbing the decks and being seasick.

When I was fourteen I had the misfortune to go on a camping holiday to Bridlington for a week. It rained every day and one day I went out on a fishing trip. Talk about being sick and wanting to die! The Navy was bang out.

After I had kicked the Navy into touch Austin immediately suggested the RAF. It looked as if he had made up our minds regarding joining up.

I gave his latest suggestion careful thought for a minute or two and came to a conclusion something like this. If I didn't join the RAF it would only be a matter of time before I would be bunged into the army. I had seen films about the First World War of soldiers being mowed down in their thousands with overfed generals miles behind the lines looking at maps and saying, 'We can afford to lose a few thousand here and a few thousand there.' So I was afraid the army wasn't for me.

Yes, the RAF sounded fine, and off we went to the recruiting office at the Mechanics' Institute on Tyrell Street.

I felt sure they would be able to find me a nice little job in the cookhouse or painting aeroplanes in the summer. Talk about living in a fool's paradise.

When we arrived at the recruiting office there was a queue of young lads like ourselves who looked as if they didn't know if they were coming or going. The atmosphere was like being in a lift, there was no conversation whatsoever. Maybe, like me, they were wondering if they were doing the right thing.

There was a row of trestle tables with an officer and a sergeant sat behind each table. At the first table they asked you questions on such things as your occupation, education, your father's occupation, your religion and why you wanted to join the RAF.

On the last question I told a pack of lies; on the other questions, owing to me still being wet behind the ears, I told the truth. I found out later that if I had told them in the proper accent that my father was a bank manager and I was at university reading the sexual habits of the African spider I would have been sent to an officer's training school. There was such a panic on at the time for recruits that they didn't have the time to check up. Maybe that is why sometimes you got a decent down to earth officer instead of the public schoolboy type.

The last table in the row was the tricky one – the medical officer. We were told to strip off; some of the lads were embarrassed and held their hands over their wedding tackle. It didn't bother me as I was used to the coarse humour of the rugby dressing room.

First of all you sat on a stool and cocked one leg over the other. The MO then tapped you on the leg just below the knee and if your foot jumped up in the air it proved that you were alive (and kicking). You then had to stand up and, without any warning, he grabbed your testicles and said, 'Cough.' and if your balls jumped up into your lower abdomen you were fit enough to be shot at by the enemy. The final part of the checkup was for you to turn round and bend down, he then seemed to concentrate for about two minutes on my ring piece. I don't know what he was looking for but by the way he walked and his tone of voice maybe he had a thing about young men's rectums.

At the end all they said was they would let us know.

When we got outside Austin said, 'It will be months before we hear anything.' He would never have made a fortune-teller. All this happened on the Saturday.

After my tea on Monday I strolled down to Austin's, it was a lovely evening, on my way I was thinking we would go to Horton Park and watch the old men playing bowls. It wasn't so much the bowls we enjoyed but we used to sit with some staunch members of the Communist Party and listen to them putting the world to rights. Two of them had fought on the side of the Red Brigade in the Spanish Civil War. Their theories and ideals were sound enough but impossible to put into practice owing to a failing in us humans called greed.

All was doom and gloom when I entered Austin's house, his mother was crying and his sisters were saying nothing, which was unusual for them. The first words his mother said as I walked in were, 'You bloody fools!' She had lost two brothers in the First World War.

Austin had received his call-up papers that morning; one day was all it had taken. The post was much quicker then than it is now. He had to report to the Mechanics' Institute on Wednesday morning with his towel and soap. I didn't see Austin for a long time.

When I got home from work on the Tuesday my mother greeted me with the news that I had got my papers. She wasn't crying, she had only lost one brother in the First World War.

I was off on Thursday; what a week that was. It's amazing how your destiny can be decided in a few days.

'Report to the Mechanics' Institute on Thursday July 18th at 9am with your towel and soap.'

At the Institute there was a group of lads like myself just stood about waiting for nobody knew what. Some of us had a little brown paper parcel, others had a small attaché case; we found out later these types were the pyjama boys.

While we were waiting I was thinking back to Tuesday morning when Mr Young, my boss, had asked me where I had been on the Monday. When I told him what I had done he was in a state of shock for about two minutes and then he started with 'God strike me. You don't know what you've done, and don't you realise that you might get killed?' and so on, until he ran out of words. After he had calmed down and got his breath back he said, 'But it will do you good.' I couldn't see how getting killed would do me good and anyway you yourself never get killed, that is something that happens to the others.

After about half an hour a chap in uniform with three stripes and a clipboard under his arm appeared.

'Right lads, when you hear your name called, answer and go over to that wall at the far end of the room. The first name on his list was Abrahams so it wouldn't be long before he got to the Ds for Davidson. Abrahams answered 'Here sir.' The man with the stripes seemed a bit annoyed at this but managed to keep himself under control as we hadn't signed the piece of paper yet. In a calm but stern tone of voice he informed us that he was a sergeant and 'not a bloody officer.' He worked his way through the rest of the names and found there were more on his list than had reported.

He didn't say where we were going, just 'Follow me and try not to get lost.'

It was only about three hundred yards to the Exchange Station so no one got lost. I bet some of them wished that they had in the years to come.

At the station there was plenty of activity going on, with lots of smoke, steam and soot filling the air.

The sergeant told us to stay where we were by the bookstall and not to wander off. He seemed frightened to death he was going to lose someone, maybe he was on commission.

After a while he came and told us to proceed to platform four from where the train to Manchester would be leaving at 10:47. In those days 10:47 meant 10:47 on the dot. The engine drivers were fanatical about punctuality.

On our travel warrants it said that we were going to Padgate which no one had ever heard of. One lad, who was braver than the rest, plucked up courage and asked the sergeant. He said he had been there lots of times but fortunately had caught the next train back. One of the older chaps that had been a long distance wagon driver said it was somewhere near Warrington.

The only time I had been on a train before was when my dad had sometimes taken me on a day trip to Ilkley in the summer holidays, so going to Manchester seemed quite a long journey.

3
England

On the way, I got chatting to a lad from Bradford called Henry Fenwick. Just for the sake of making conversation I asked if he liked sport, his abrupt answer was no, so I asked him what he did on Saturday afternoons and he replied, ‘I’m married.’ It took me a while to work that one out but later on, when I got to know Henry better, I knew what he meant.

On arriving at Manchester we had to change trains and go to another station, it was nearly half a mile away and when we got there we found that we were on the same platform as we had just been on. One knowledge box in our group explained to us that it was the longest platform in Britain and went from one station to the other; what puzzled me was why we didn’t just walk along the platform from one station to the other.

Another wait and then the train for Padgate arrived and by this time a large number of groups of other lads had arrived. Each group had their very own sergeant who then got into a little group of their own and looked to be having a good laugh. Looking around I couldn’t see much to laugh about apart from us.

It wasn’t a long way from Padgate railway station to the camp gates so no one went missing; it would have been difficult for anyone to go missing with our three-striped guardian angel running around like a Welsh sheepdog.

And then there it was – the main gate. Up went the pole with the weight on one end. The two airmen operating the pole had a kind of cynical smile on their faces as they let us through. They both had a rifle slung on their shoulder, which disturbed me as I had only seen rifles before in films and besides that I always thought airmen had aeroplanes and soldiers had guns.

I had a lot to learn, which I did in the next few months at the speed of sound.

Huts! There were huts as far as my eyes could see; after fifty yards or so along the street between the huts the sergeant counted off the leading twenty of us and handed us over to a chap with two stripes, who on the day after we found to our sorrow was a corporal. The sergeant left us and hurried off towards the main gate as if he had a train to catch.

The corporal, who gave the impression of being a nice chap, asked us to follow him. Eventually we came to a hut that was to be our abode for the next two nights. There were only three of us in the hut from the group that had left Bradford. There was the married man Fenwick, me, and the other was a lad called McCabe.

The beds had three two foot square mattresses stacked up at the top end of the bed that when laid out made a bed six foot by two foot, folded up on top of the 'biscuits', as the mattresses were called, were two army blankets and a canvas pillow.

On the bed to my left was a man from Edinburgh who was twenty-seven and had pyjamas; on my right was a lad from Hull who had worked on a trawler. He was eighteen but looked older and was a bit of a ruffian, so we palled up straight away. Being a fisherman was an exempted occupation, so he had told them at the recruiting office he was a bookie's runner. Ronnie Kirby and I were good pals for the next year or two.

Nothing happened for the rest of the day and no one told us anything, so we just sat around chatting. Most of the conversation seemed to be about their sexual activities with girls, and as I had never been out with a girl I kept my mouth shut.

A few of the more adventurous types went for a walk around the camp and after a while they came back and told us they had found a place known as the NAAFI. This was a canteen where we could get a cup of tea and a rock bun for two pence, so Ronnie and I wandered off to sample the delights of this famous institution.

The tea wasn't so bad, I have had worse but not much. As for the rock buns they were unique. In time to come, as I travelled the world, I discovered that the rock buns in all the NAAFIs were exactly the same. As the name implies they were as hard as rocks, exactly the same size and if you cared to count the currants there was exactly the same number whether you were in Bombay or Benghazi.

When we got back to the hut we were told the nice friendly corporal had been to tell us tea was being served in the cookhouse at four-thirty and we could find our own way there. After a lot of walking about and asking for directions we eventually found it. Some of the old sweats who had been in for two or three weeks directed us the wrong way just for a laugh.

For tea we had sausage, mash and beans followed by jam roly-poly with custard, finished off with a nice pot of tea. Ronnie and I thought it was great but some of the pyjama brigade couldn't eat theirs so we had extra sausages. Things were looking better than I expected.

There was a cinema on the camp and that was where we went on our first night. It always seems strange to me how one can remember little things after sixty-five years. I can even remember the film, it was Tyrone Power and Henry Fonda in the cowboy picture 'Jesse James'.

Off to bed for the first night; to say there was plenty of snoring going on and talking in their sleep I didn't have a bad night. Most of the talking was between the married men and their wives.

The next morning we were up bright and early, well early anyway. It wasn't bad for me as I was used to getting up before seven. The ablutions were just across the road from the hut, so after a wash (no shave, as I hadn't started to grow whiskers yet), it was off to the cookhouse again.

Porridge, bacon, beans and fried bread washed down with a good pot of tea. With grub like this I would soon be growing whiskers.

At 10 o'clock the corporal came into the hut and asked us to follow him.

He took us to another hut that was much larger than the others. Inside there were about two hundred lads standing in lines. At the top end of the room were two tables covered with blankets. On one table there was a Bible, a pile of forms and a pen and ink bottle facing towards us, on the other table was a heap of shillings. Behind the clerical table was an officer and a sergeant, behind the shilling table were two sergeants and a warrant officer. One of the sergeants was an SP (service policeman). Maybe at some time in the past an enterprising recruit had tried to run away with the shillings.

One by one we went up to the tables and swore on the Bible that we were willing to die for our King and Country. I was glad it didn't apply to me as it was a Church of England Bible and I was a Roman Catholic. In fact, according to our old parish priest, had I signed it with genuine intentions and got killed I would go straight to hell, and in any case the last thing on my mind was to get killed for King, Country or any other Tom, Dick or Harry. So I signed the form, took the shilling and went on my way rejoicing like the thieves and the Samaritan in the parable 'On the road to Damascus'. For the aid of readers who have been deprived of a religious upbringing a part of it goes something like this.

'And it came to pass that he fell among thieves, not common thieves but arse thieves, and they ragged him, bagged him and shagged him and went on their way rejoicing.'

That was it, I was in, for what they called the duration of the present emergency. Which if I had thought about it seriously wouldn't be long as the Germans were winning hands down and were going to invade our green and pleasant land at any minute.

The next job was getting kitted out. Another hut, but much bigger than the last one, and another queue. It came to my mind that up until now we had spent about fifty per cent of our time in queues.

No wonder wars go on for years. It made me feel glad I hadn't been in the hundred-year war, just imagine standing in queues for fifty years.

Through the door was a long line of tables joined together to make the longest counter that I had ever seen, and behind the counter was a large number of airmen who I found out later were known as store bashers. I also found out later that store bashers made very good friends, even if you didn't like them.

Behind the store bashers were lots of shelves containing what were to be all my worldly goods for the next few years.

The first man behind the counter called out a number and that was your size from braces to bootlaces. There was a sergeant with a clipboard and as each item of equipment was thrown across the table at you he marked it off on a sheet of paper containing your name and number.

I forgot to mention earlier that we were given our number at the swearing in bit, my number was 1060076. You never forget your service number or your rifle number even if you live to be 86. As for the rifle number, I had no intention at the time of having a rifle for the simple reason that if you fire a gun at someone there is a strong possibility they will fire back at you. Little did I know then that I would spend the next six years with a rifle as my bedmate.

We went back to the billet carrying lots of things under our arms and dragging our kitbags behind us.

Back in the billet we piled all the kit on our beds and waited for the corporal who arrived eventually with the camp tailor. I was beginning to find there were some lovely jobs in the Air Force if you were lucky.

The order from the corporal was, 'Right lads, get your new suits on and be quick about it.' We couldn't be that quick as we were still in our civvies. I was fortunate to have a uniform that fitted me.

The tailor made chalk marks here and there on the uniforms of the ones that didn't fit, told them to get changed back into their civvies and follow him to the tailor's shop where they would be made to fit and be ready for tomorrow morning.

That night a few of us went to the NAAFI where I had my first pint of NAAFI beer. One of the lads that was with us could play the piano and he played a piece called the *Poet and Peasant*. It was the first time in my life I had listened to any classical music and I really enjoyed it.

The next morning we were given a sheet of brown paper and a piece of string and told to parcel up our civvies, put our home address on the label and throw it on the cart with the others; it must have made our parents feel sad when the parcels reached home.

After dinner, which was the midday meal in those days, unless you were posh and then dinner was at teatime, some NCOs from the permanent staff herded about 200 of us together and drove us like sheep to the railway station.

Eventually the train arrived; puffing, groaning, rattling and belching out clouds of steam. All aboard and off we went.

No one seemed to know where we were going but I heard a

sergeant saying something about having a pint in the sergeants' mess that night so it didn't look as if we were going a long way.

I don't remember much about the journey except that when we got off the train we got on a bus and finally arrived at a training camp at West Kirby on the Wirral peninsula between Birkenhead and Chester.

With my extensive knowledge of geography at the time we could have been on the moon and I wouldn't have known.

More huts. We were counted off into twenties by the men with stripes on their sleeves who let it be known straight away that we could be their friends or their enemies, but if we chose to be their enemies it would be a case of 'God help us'. The trouble with this caper, we were soon to find out, was it only worked one way and it wasn't our way.

Twenty of us were dumped into each hut where we first sorted ourselves out with beds as that seemed to be the most important item after our long day.

My pal Ronnie and I and the other lads that slept in their shirts finished up at one end of the hut and the pyjama boys at the other end. It is strange how class distinction falls into place. Looking back, I sometimes wonder if it was us in our shirts who were the snobs.

The three week's training was amazing. In those three weeks they taught us how to march, fire a rifle and most important of all, how to salute an officer. We were confined to camp for the first two weeks in case we happened to bump into one and didn't salute him properly.

We had our very own corporal who had his own little room at the end of the hut. He cursed and bullied us for the three weeks of our stay and at bayonet practice he kept on telling us that once we had drawn blood we would crave for more. I wondered if he had ever cut his finger.

Then there were the inoculations that they gave us on Saturday morning so we could get over the pain and fever in our time off on Saturday afternoon and Sunday, and be ready for action again on Monday morning.

After all this we clubbed together and bought the corporal a cigarette lighter. With all the trainees that passed through West Kirby every three weeks he must have had a sack full of cigarette lighters in his little room at the end of the hut.

When our three weeks was up we came to the passing out parade. It was such a scorching hot day that some of the lads passed out before the commanding officer had said his passing out speech.

A day or so before the passing out parade the corporal gave us all a form to fill in which asked us to put where we would like to be posted to at the end of our training. Everybody was trying to work out the nearest Air Force station to their home town. Our corporal had a quiet word and told us the powers that be would send you as far away as possible from what we put on the form, so I put 'anywhere'.

On August the 17th, sixty of us were detailed to get into full marching order and on the parade ground in ten minutes. Why the rush no one knew, as we were standing on the parade ground with the August sun beating down on our heads for over an hour waiting for no one knew what.

At last a sergeant and two corporals arrived and marched us off to the station where we boarded a train and off we went.

One of the brighter lads, who had been in the Boy Scouts and could tell the time by the sun, tie knots and fend off mad dogs with his pole, said we were heading south east.

At about 2pm we arrived at Hucknall, a small town north of Nottingham.

The sergeant marched us from the station to an airfield on the outskirts of the town. On seeing an aeroplane on the ground for the first time in my life I was a bit disappointed by how small they were. When I got to know more about aircraft I found they were Hurricanes and Fairy Battles. The Fairy Battle was the biggest single engined aircraft that Britain had at the time.

Having stood for another hour or so with the sun beating down on us it turned out we were at the wrong camp. Nothing seemed to be happening, when all of sudden some three ton wagons came along and took us to a little village about two miles away called Watnall. In the centre of the village was a camp known as '12 Group Headquarters Fighter Command' where I did some hard work but had some happy times.

On arriving at Watnall we stood around in an untidy group outside what I found out later was the Guardroom, which I became very familiar with later on in my stay at Watnall.

There was no one about except a couple of WAAFs who

walked past and looked at us like we were a prize in a raffle. Not surprisingly, for we found out later that up to us arriving there had been 200 WAAFs on the camp and about 50 airmen.

A flight sergeant appeared on the scene and we all sprang to attention. He was an old man who looked to be in his forties and he had medal ribbons on his tunic from the First World War. He took one look at us and in a quiet tone of voice he said, 'You look knackered so take your packs off, sit on the grass and I will go to the cookhouse and arrange some tea.' These were the first kind words that we had heard for nearly a month; his name was Flight Sergeant Burridge and for the remainder of our stay at Watnall he was like a father to us.

What a shock greeted us in the cookhouse, bread and butter on plates, fish chips and peas followed by strawberries and cream served by pretty WAAFs; they were forced to look pretty as we hadn't seen any females for four weeks.

Chiefy (slang for flight sergeant) then took us to our sleeping quarters which was six bell tents in a little field at the top end of the camp; it was ten men to a tent; with the tents being circular we slept with our feet to the pole that was in the centre of the tent. If the man who slept furthest away from the entrance came in late or off a middle of the night guard it caused a lot of cursing and swearing; we didn't stay in the tents long as there were some workmen already building our huts opposite the cookhouse.

The next morning, after breakfast, we paraded outside the guardroom and received a pep talk from the defence officer. He gave me the impression of being a prize pratt; he only had one arm, with the other, by all accounts, being lost in a motoring accident. He held the rank of pilot officer without the pilots' wings and had medal ribbons from the First War. He informed us that the Germans were going to invade our green and pleasant land at any minute and that all leave was cancelled for an indefinite period. We had to sort ourselves out into groups of three and the eldest in the group would be issued with a rifle and ten rounds of ammunition and the other two with pick shafts.

I think that the idea was that whilst the man with the rifle was keeping the Nazi's attention occupied with his gun, we had to creep up behind him and clout him on the head with our pick shafts, or something like that.

Our threesome was my pal Ronnie, a Geordie called Charlie

Bartrem and myself. I had by now acquired the nickname of Dave, it was amazing how soon we were given nicknames. Charlie, being the eldest, was in charge of the rifle.

The three of us were taken to a barn on the outskirts of the village; there was a hole in one wall looking away from the village that gave us a good view over some open fields.

We were in that barn for three days and three nights; now and again two WAAFs brought us some food from the cookhouse, but not very often.

The first night was the worst.

It was a typical summer night with enough moon for us to be able to make out the shape of the trees and hedgerows.

We had decided to do two hours on and four hours off watching out through the hole, with the one on watch rousing the other two should something happen. Ronnie and I had just dozed off to sleep when Charlie shook us awake and told us to be quiet at the same time. He whispered, 'There is someone at the bottom of the field.' We looked through the hole in the wall and sure enough there at the bottom of the field was what looked like a figure with two legs, a head and a pack on its back. After a hasty confab about what we should do, Charlie decided that we should do what we had been told, which was shout in a loud and clear voice, 'Halt, who goes there?' On the third shout without a reply it changes to 'Halt, or I fire.' There was no reply and I was thanking the Lord above that it was Charlie that had the rifle and not me. I heard him pull the bolt back and push it forward then there was an almighty bang. He'd missed and the figure at the bottom of the field jumped up in the air and landed sideways on. It was a horse, and off it went looking as if it was in the last furlong at Ascot. We heard later that it had been found wandering about on the main street in Hucknall.

What a commotion. There were voices shouting from all over the place, 'Turn out the guard, they're here'; all because of one shot.

I dreaded to think what would happen when they did arrive.

The following morning the defence officer came to the barn and he brusquely told us that we were lucky not to be on a court martial for firing a rifle without his permission.

This order carried on for a while until one night there was a bad air raid (not that there were any good air raids) and we didn't get the order to open fire as the ones that were to give the order had taken shelter under the billiard table in the officers' mess.

Joe Pickup, the barman in the mess, kept us up to date with the activities of our superiors.

The night that the Germans bombed Coventry I was on a machine gun post at the top of a tower on a covered-in reservoir. This reservoir was on top of a hill behind the camp and from there we could see a great red glow in the sky to the west, forty miles away. It was Coventry burning.

The German planes were droning overhead on their way to their target, we opened fire but there was no chance of hitting them at ten thousand feet or so. We had by this time been given the order to fire at our own discretion; this gave us the excitement of firing the twin Lewis guns and allowed the ones in command to stay in their hidey holes under the billiard table.

In a week or two the flight sergeant sorted thing out into a routine that went something like this.

Guard duties on the gun posts were two hours on and four hours off for twenty-four hours. The guard was changed at fourteen hundred hours each day. When we came off guard on the following day we had the afternoon and the night off. The next morning we did foot drill, rifle drill, lessons on various machine guns, barbed wiring etc., until fourteen hundred hours when it was time to go on guard again. This went on and on without a break owing to the threat of imminent German invasion.

A few nights after the Coventry raid they came and had a go at Nottingham. A bomb dropped on a house not far away from the camp. The next morning, which happened to be my morning on drill, Chiefy asked for six volunteers to go and help to clean up the mess in the house, as there had been two people in the front room when the bomb dropped.

It was the usual method used in asking for volunteers which always ended up with 'You, you and you.' I was the first you.

Our orders were to go into the house and put the bodies into a couple of coffins that the local joiner had knocked together. The house was still standing but in a bit of a mess. The police were in attendance and had cordoned the area off.

In we went. It was a minute or two before I could recognise anything resembling a house, everywhere was dust and rubble. We searched half-heartedly amongst the bricks and bits of furniture. The biggest bit of body I found was an arm and hand with an engagement ring on the third finger. If this was what war was all about, I didn't like it. Two of the lads were sick and it surprised me that I wasn't, although I felt as if I could have been.

One morning on drill parade Chiefy tried us out at giving the orders. The four that he chose as best were promoted to the rank of corporal; he must have been a good judge as all four of them turned out to be right nasty sods.

At that time we were known as station defence but after a while that was changed to ground gunners for which we wore a badge on our sleeve with the letters GG. The ground gunner outfits didn't last long before they became the RAF Regiment.

One Sunday morning we had an exercise with the Home Guard; they were going to capture the camp so our defence officer spread us out to surround the camp. That was just the men that were not on guard duty, they were told to take no part in the exercise. Our little group was positioned on a railway embankment to the southeast of the camp. It was a lovely Indian summer morning and we soon got settled down in the long grass. We had been told that if nothing had happened by twelve o'clock we were to make our way back.

When we got back the Home Guard had taken over the camp. They had gained entry by concealing themselves in the back of the laundry van that always came on a Sunday morning to collect our dirty washing. When the van pulled up in the middle of the communal site they had all jumped out and captured the camp. As time went on I think we improved; we couldn't have got any worse but it took some living down in the local pubs.

November came along and Adolph Hitler had decided not to invade Britain for some reason; nobody found out why, unless it was losing the Battle of Britain that put him off. Maybe he thought the Home Guard (Dads' Army) was much bigger than it was, or maybe he thought that we would go in with him against Russia, which Mr Churchill might have done if the British working class would have stood for it.

We had another pleasant surprise in November when it came up on orders that we could all have a forty-eight hour leave pass; it wasn't practical for us all to go at the time, so the people in charge decided that it would be spread over three weekends for which we drew lots by picking bits of paper out of a cap. This seemed to be the method of deciding most things; in fact it was so popular that most likely it was the way that the generals used when deciding whether to advance or retreat.

It wasn't my lucky day and I got the third week, although that didn't turn out so bad in the long run. The forty-eight hour pass started after coming off guard duties on the Friday at fourteen hundred hours.

On Thursday the married men and some of the single optimists were running around looking for condoms or 'rubber Johnnies' as they were called in those days. One chap even got into the chemist's shop, but it was a lady behind the counter and he came out with a bottle of aspirins!

This gave me an idea, for in my wanderings around Nottingham in my time off I had noticed a seedy looking little shop behind the Parish Church that, going by the window display, sold nothing else but baby blockers, so off I went to Nottingham with my last two shillings in my pocket. I walked it there and back because if you are going into business one can't be wasting money on bus fares.

After I had sat on a bench for about twenty minutes plucking up courage to go into the shop and freezing from my toes upwards, in I went hoping that it would be a man behind the counter, but no, it was a sweet young thing of about eighteen summers. I could blush if a girl looked at me on a bus, so that afternoon my face must have looked like a bullfighter's cape.

In for a penny, in for a pound, so trying to put on a confident man about town manner I asked the price of the ones on the nearest shelf, they were called Paragon Sheaths. 'Three half pence each… ' said the girl and with a cheeky grin on her face '…they're cheaper if you buy a gross.' (That's 144!)

While being conscious of my embarrassment I was at the same time trying to work out how many three half pennies there was in two shillings, after a bit more mental arithmetic I said, 'Alright, I'll have sixteen.' She took my money and gave me a funny look and off I went falling over the doormat on my way out of the shop.

Back at the camp it took me less than ten minutes to sell the lot at four pence each; I think that I could have asked for more if I hadn't relied on the old Jewish concept of a small profit and a quick turnover. Three shillings and four pence wasn't a bad profit when all that I was getting for my pay was two shillings a day out of which I allowed my mother a shilling.

My business was flourishing and I became known on the camp as 'Dave the French letter king'. I also got to know the girl in the shop quite well. I think she knew what my game was or maybe she thought I was a stud stallion. There were times when I was on the verge of asking her for a date but I was either too shy or I thought that a nice girl like her wouldn't want to go out with the likes of me.

As I write this now it makes me think how things have changed since those days. Now, every time I switch on the television there are usually animals fornicating or couples jumping into bed and they're not always of the opposite sex. And condoms scattered about the school playgrounds like spent balloons after a Christmas party. On the other hand, it was just the same then but it all went on behind drawn curtains and in air raid shelters.

Eventually it came round to my turn to go home for the weekend. I collected my 295 (leave pass) and travel warrant and was on my way to Bradford.

There was a chap in our hut called Henry who came from Bradford and had been home on the first weekend. Henry was a droll character of whom I could never tell if he was being serious or taking the piss. When he came back from his weekend leave he went to great lengths telling me that our fair and soot shrouded city of Bradford had been flattened by enemy bombs.

Going in on the train I could see the town hall clock and all the other buildings that had been there before I went away, so I wondered if Henry had been using his warped sense of humour on me.

The city had had a few bombs on it but nothing compared with cities like Hull and Sheffield etc. It was said by the know-alls that it was an error of navigation as there were so many mills and wool warehouses in Bradford owned by Germans that they must have mistaken it for Heckmondwike or somewhere like that.

The weekend passed without anything exciting happening; I think the family were glad to see me.

While I had been away my brother had got married and the happy couple were now sharing the bed that my brother and I had always slept in, so I had to sleep on the floor downstairs. In a way I was glad to get back to the camp; it is amazing how quickly we can become institutionalised.

It wasn't long after coming back from my weekend leave that I was put on my first charge (form 252). It was for telling Corporal Jopling to go and have sexual intercourse with himself. The charge was insubordination.

The next morning I was up in front of the CO, he kept looking at the charge sheet with a puzzled expression; it seemed as if he was wondering how it was possible to perform such an act.

I got seven days confined to camp. Whilst doing my seven days a clever fellow from Northern Ireland called Paddy Rowan asked where I got the condoms from; I told him a second hand shop in John O'Groats down a little back street.

My next charge was for delaying an officer in the course of his duties. What happened was that one of the sentry posts was down a passageway, then a flight of steps led down to an operation bunker where WAAFs round a big table pushed about little aeroplanes whose height and direction were relayed to them from observation posts located on the east coast.

Anyone coming down the passage had to be commanded to halt and asked for the password that was changed at eighteen hundred hours each day. The system that we used for finding out the new password was to ask the first person that came down the passage after six o'clock; the first one that evening was a WAAF and she answered 'cabbage' so I let her through; the next person down the passage was a flying officer who answered 'cauliflower'.

At first I was at a loss what to do and the officer was calling me all kinds of things in his posh accent, and I found out that the word bastard has an 'o' and 'r' in it and is pronounced borstard. While he was ranting on another WAAF came along, gave the password as 'cauliflower' and identified the officer as one of her superiors. About ten minutes later two Service Police (SP) turned up with a relief guard to take my place.

Off I was marched to the cell in the guardroom that was all spick and span as I was its first occupant. At ten o'clock the SP corporal on duty came and asked me if I would like to help him with signing people in who had been out for the night and have a chat and a pot of tea. I also had a night in bed that I wouldn't have got if I had been on guard.

The next morning I was up in front of the CO again; he read the charge out to me and asked me what I had to say for myself, which wasn't much; he made a note about altering the method that we had been using for obtaining the password and gave me a seven-day detention.

For seven days you did it on your own camp; if it had been fourteen days or over I would have been sent to a glasshouse such as Garrison Prison at Hull, that by all accounts would have been hell on earth. There was a tale went round that one lad who did twenty-eight days in there came out with part of his hair turned white.

They put me in the cell and at dinnertime an SP called Corporal Bell took me under escort to the cookhouse. I was the centre of attraction and went to the front of the queue where the girls serving the food must have felt sorry for me and gave me extra large helpings. We had a table to ourselves and Cpl. Bell helped me out with what I couldn't eat; he was a big lad. That afternoon I scrubbed the guardroom floor, had my tea, helped with the signing in again and had another night in bed.

The next morning the Cpl. took me to a lane behind the camp in my full pack to give me pack drill for a half hour. We doubled round to the lane, he ordered me to take my pack off and we sat on a wall for a half hour watching the sun rise over the huts.

After breakfast, with my full pack on again, Cpl. Bell double marched me down to a piece of spare land at the side of the football field. I also had with me a pick and shovel, which didn't make me feel too happy as it was a warm day for that time of the year.

As part of my punishment I had to dig holes, six foot by three foot and about six foot deep, which at the time seemed a bit soul destroying but I supposed that was part of the punishment. So I marked one out and got digging. The Cpl. selected himself a nice spot behind the hedge and sat down with a paperback novel, resting his back against a grassy bank. When I had got part way down the hole he said 'Right Dave.' and fished another novel out of his pocket and I settled down beside the Cpl. until lunchtime. All I had to do was keep awake in case the Cpl. nodded off to sleep.

As the novel was a saucy one for those days (*No Orchids for Miss Blandish*) I didn't find it a problem to keep my eyes open. It was the second book that I had read in my life; it looked like my education was coming on in leaps and bounds. Cpl. Bell and I became good pals.

It was coming on to Christmas now and they told us that we could have seven days' leave spread over three weeks so we drew lots; I was lucky this time as I drew Christmas week.

There was a lad in our hut called Bob Smith who came from Nelson in Lancashire. He was one of the older ones, aged about twenty-four, and the stories that were going around about my escapades worried him a bit as I was only eighteen. It's strange how people always think the worst about you once the tongues start wagging. One night I had stayed out all night owing to the buses having stopped running because of an air raid. In a matter of two or three hours it was all round the camp that I had slept out with a woman in Nottingham. What really happened was that I had slept on the top deck of a bus outside the bus depot and nearly froze to death. Telling this to the CO didn't stop me getting another seven days confined to camp.

One day Bob must have thought that it was about time that someone tried to get me on the straight and narrow, so he asked me if I fancied going with him and his girlfriend to a dance at the Miners' Welfare Club at Hill Top, a little place between Watnall and Eastwood. More or less every village had a Miners' Welfare for at that time coal mines were in abundance in that area.

I had no idea about dancing but he did mention a bar so I was interested. With me always having money in my pocket from my little business I was downing about four pints a night on my nights off that were spent mostly in a pub called the Nelson and Railway in Kimberley, another little mining village near Watnall.

When we got to the Miners' Welfare, Bob introduced me to his girlfriend. Her name was Annie and she had a friend with her called Alice. I asked them to have a drink; it was a half of beer for Bob, lemonade for the girls and a pint of beer for me, and that was all we had all night. I couldn't see the club lasting for long with customers like us.

As I wasn't making any advances to Alice regarding the dancing caper, she eventually asked me if I would like to have a dance. I was beginning to realise that Bob had set up the meeting, which surprised me as Alice was quite an attractive girl, but a bit old for me at twenty-one, and did not already have a boyfriend. I told her that I had never danced before and wouldn't know how to begin.

She tried to show me some basic steps; I found that I had two left feet and had the feeling that everybody was watching us. What made thing worse was that I had never been held in a woman's arms since I was about two years old and it gave me a kind of a funny feeling.

Alice never asked me to go dancing again although we went for walks and to the cinema. After we had been out together two or three times she took me home to meet her parents and I got my feet under the table, which made a nice change on the winter nights from drinking with the locals at the Nelson and Railway.

Mr Taylor, Alice's father, worked at the mine at Moor Green and was a lay preacher at the local chapel on Sundays. Alice worked in Boots store in Nottingham and they lived in a detached house on Dovecote Road, Hilltop. They had a Welsh sheepdog that we took for walks, then back home for supper in front of a nice fire, a kiss and a cuddle and back to camp. It was the first time that I had ever kissed a girl so it meant taking lessons from Alice. It would have shocked the lads at the camp if they had known this about Dave the philanderer. I had seen it on films about people falling madly in love and all that. We were very comfortable in each other's company but I never felt that I was walking on air or anything like that.

In May we had finally got over a dreadful winter; it must have been bad because they had been giving us a tablespoonful of rum before we went on guard and allowed us to have braziers in the gun pits covered over by a sheet of metal so that the fire couldn't be seen from the air.

My conduct had improved. I had only been in trouble once throughout the winter and that was for getting caught stealing coal from the compound for which I got seven days confined to camp. It had been so cold that the weekly ration of coal for the stove in the hut never lasted the week out.

May came along and the winter was over. The air raids had eased off and everything looked rosy, then on one sunny morning when we went on parade, his first words, even before he brought us to attention were: 'Dave, go get your kit packed, you're moving. After you've packed your kit go to the orderly room and get your travel warrant.'

As I was packing I was thinking of all the nasty places that I had heard about like Wick, Iceland and the Orkney Islands etc.

I handed my rifle in at the armoury and went to the orderly room. The WAAF that gave me my travel warrant said that she hoped I would like where I was going, that frightened me more than ever as I sensed a touch of sarcasm in her remark. Another thing that made me nervous was that I had never travelled by myself before, when I didn't know where I was going.

All it said on the instructions was 'train to Lincoln, bus to Digby'. I had never heard of the place, but having got a lift on a wagon to Nottingham I thought that I was doing fine. I had to wait about two hours in Lincoln before I finally got the bus to Digby. I found out later that I had been lucky as there were only three buses a day and it seemed to travel three times around Lincolnshire before it reached Digby.

On arriving the SP Sgt. told me to leave my kit in the guardroom and go for some tea. It was the first bite to eat that I had had since breakfast. After tea the Sgt. took me to the communal quarters, fixed me up with a bed for the night and told me to report to the orderly room in the morning.

After sorting my kit out and listening to the old sweats telling me what a rotten place it was and that the food in the cookhouse wasn't fit for pigs, I found Digby very pleasant. The food was good and everything about the place suited me fine. After listening to them for a while I got fed up with their moaning and decided to have a walk round the airfield.

I had never seen an airfield close to before and what fascinated me most of all was the size of the field and the hangars. There were a few Hurricanes and Spitfires on the tarmac in front of the hangars looking as if they could take off at a minute's notice. The whole set-up was new to me and looked exciting.

The following morning I had an early breakfast, found the orderly room where after a lot of sorting papers, people pointing at me and asking each other questions, a WAAF clerk came to me and told me to report to the flight sergeant at the Station Flight hangar. Nobody that I asked knew where it was. One bright spark thought that it was somewhere on the airfield. Eventually I asked a Canadian lad who said that he was going there. On the way he told me that there were two Canadian squadrons, or what was left of them, stationed here at Digby; 401 and 402 Hurricanes. He seemed a nice lad and was telling me all about his home and family in Canada. I never saw him again as a day or so later there was an air raid and a bomb dropped on a group of Canadian airmen on their way to the cook house, he was in the group.

I was lucky to find the flight sergeant, for I found out later he spent a lot of his time in the sergeants' mess. He was a Geordie, a pleasant little man and introduced himself as Chiefy.

It took him about half an hour to put me in the picture. First of all he took me to meet the gang. They were in a room built off the side of the hangar shrouded in a cloud of tobacco smoke. There was a sign on the door; STATION FLIGHT WORKSHOP. The only thing that I could see resembling a workshop was a bench by the window with a vice on it and a metal locker that I presumed had tools in it. There was a stove with a big kettle simmering on it and six grubby looking pots on a table. There were six chairs, the one nearest the door was to become mine. It didn't look too busy for a workshop but I was mistaken, I found out later that it was a hive of industry but with very little to do with aeroplanes.

In the other five chairs were five recumbent airmen who never even moved when Chiefy and I walked in. The only response, in perfect harmony, was 'Hello Chiefy'. He pointed to a life size replica of Billy Bunter who was reclining in his chair and said, 'He's your mate, he'll show you how to go on,' and with a brisk about turn off he went, no doubt back to the sergeants' mess.

One of the lads that looked as if he had a bit more about him than the others asked me my name. I told him and added that I usually answered to Dave. His name was Sykes and he was the engine fitter; there was Ruddick the airframe fitter, Jarvis the sparks and Lewis the wireless man. Tubby and I were the armourers. I couldn't understand at first why there were two armourers but I soon found out that it didn't matter as we all mucked in and helped each other, which with me not knowing the first thing about aeroplanes I really enjoyed, and it gave me the chance to learn.

The other reason for two armourers was that there always had to be someone awake, so Tubby and I did twenty-four hours on and twenty-four off. It never worked and was a bit of a laugh.

We had two Hurricanes and a Tiger Moth to look after. The pilot of one of the Hurricanes was a Group Captain Turton-Jones who was just like his name suggests. The other pilot was Wing Commander McGregor, a Canadian, who was one of nature's gentlemen. The room next to the workshop/rest room was where we slept. It had six bunk beds and a table with six more grubby pots on it with a jar of tea, a jar of sugar and a tin of condensed milk.

The next morning we went out to the dispersals to do the DIs (daily inspections) on the aircraft. Tubby and I cleaned the eight guns on each Hurricane, cocked them so that they were ready to fire and made sure that the ammunition boxes were full.

Sykes ran the engine for ten minutes or so; this involved one sitting in the cockpit at the controls and the others making sure that the chocks were under the wheels. The exciting part was when the one in the cockpit opened the throttle to do what was called 'taking the engine through the gate', which was about four thousand revs per minute. The rest of us had to drape ourselves over the tail plane to keep the back end down, holding on for dear life so as not to get blown into the next field. Sometimes Sykes would let one of us others do the engine bit.

The Tiger Moth not having any guns meant that Tubby and I just helped out with the others. The DI on the engine was a different carry on; we had to swing the propeller manually to start it.

For starting the Hurricanes we had a Coffman starter that was a big gun loaded with a blank cartridge and pushed into a socket in the cockpit. You pulled the trigger and sometimes the engine started.

The first time Sykes let me have a go in the cockpit was more exciting than when I had my first blow through.

The rest of the days we spent making little Spitfire brooches out of pennies in our workshop, or if it was a nice day we would just laze about in the sun on the dispersals.

One peaceful afternoon, when I had just dozed off to sleep, the roar of engines awakened me and all of a sudden two of Goering's playthings came out of nowhere and started strafing the airfield and haphazardly dropping a few bombs. In one swift movement we all shot down into the air raid shelter that was underneath the earth mound that went round three sides of the dispersal. After a while, when we had got our breath back, Tubby, who was standing next to me in the dark, gave me a push and said, 'Move up, I'm stood in a pool of water.' A voice in the dark said, 'You can't be stood in water, it hasn't rained for a month.' Ruddick, who was the other side of Tubby, struck a match to have a look and, lo and behold, there was a trickle of blood running out of Tubby's right boot. A bullet had nicked his right shin.

When the raid was over and we got him back into the workshop we washed it and put a dressing on it and he was as right as rain. I don't think that he got a wound stripe for it.

One morning Sykes and I were mooching about on the airfield looking for butterfly bombs; they were a small bomb that the Luftwaffe had started dropping on airfields during the night; they looked like an empty soup or vegetable tin. The idea was that lads going out on to the airfield at six o'clock in the morning to work on the aircraft, half asleep and feeling grumpy, would give the tin a kick and BANG! They would lose whichever foot they used to kick a football with.

On the field there were lots of big brown juicy mushrooms. Like small minds do as well as great minds, when there is money to be made, we both immediately had the same thought. Sykes had a friend in Metheringham, a village near Digby, who he had done one or two shady dealings with, not that this one was shady (not yet anyway). He also had a motorbike.

The petrol used in the Hurricanes was high-octane stuff; if it had been used in a car the valves would have burnt out in no time. The fuel for the Tiger Moth was ordinary petrol with a red dye in it and could be used in cars as long as they didn't break the eleventh commandment (thou shall not get caught). It came in four-gallon tins that were packed in a cardboard box that would be just the ticket for transporting the mushrooms in.

The next morning we went to Metheringham with a box of mushrooms perched on the petrol tank between Sykes and the handlebars and me on the pillion holding on for dear life, as I had never had the thrill of clinging to the rear end of a motorbike before.

We had to pass the guardroom on our exit from the camp. We stopped at the gate and a Cpl. SP came out of the guardroom. He asked us what was in the box. When we told him mushrooms, he had a look and said that he would turn a blind eye so long as we bought him a pint when we saw him in the pub. The trouble was that he seemed to be in the pub every night.

For the first morning or two he looked in our box to see that our cargo was only mushrooms. After three or four mornings he raised the barrier and waved us through. The next day the mushrooms had miraculously turned into petrol.

Times were looking good again; what money we acquired from making brooches etc., was shared out between us with Sykes getting a double share as he had the motorbike and the knack of doing business, maybe because his family had a couple of baker's shops in Norwich.

With the money that was coming in we were spending most nights in a pub in Metheringham and all we had to do was to leave one man to keep watch on the aircraft.

On an afternoon when we were lounging about on the dispersals, we sometimes saw a strange looking aircraft flying about. I say strange, this was because it didn't have an airscrew (propeller).

It puzzled us until one night in the pub a farm labourer told us it was a prototype jet plane. He explained to us the basic principles of how it worked and it struck me it was the same method I had used many times for getting birds' nests out of the top of drain pipes when I was an apprentice. What I did was soak a piece of rag in paraffin, push it loosely in the bottom of the drain pipe, set light to it and when the air in the pipe heats up it expands and whoosh! the nest and anything else blocking the pipe shoots out the top. The trouble was that if the pipe was cast iron it would sometimes crack and then I would have to tell the lady of the house it was the winter frost that had cracked it.

It goes to show what power expanding air can generate, especially when you look at the big jet engines of today and the force they produce.

We wondered at times if the farm labourer was a German spy and although there were posters all over the place telling us to watch out for fifth columnists (spies) we didn't say anything as he seemed a nice jovial kind of chap.

Another lad we got friendly with was an airman who had the cushy job as the Padre's Clerk. Every camp of any size had a Padre and every Padre had a clerk who looked after the office whilst the Padre was away attending to his spiritual duties or something like that. Any airman or WAAF who was having marital problems or whose home had been bombed would go to the Padre for counselling and a spot of compassionate leave. One night in the pub it came out in the conversation that there was a pile of 295s (leave forms) stacked neatly on a shelf in the Padre's office.

Next morning, after our petrol run, the conversation in the flight workshop was all about forging passes and what it would cost to induce the Padre's clerk to let us have a hundred now and again. Ruddick was against the idea on the grounds that the clerk may be honest. Sykes argued how could a chap wangle a job like that and be honest and anyway, everyone has a price.

Another problem was the orderly room stamp that had to be on every pass. I came up with the idea of a light box, which I could make out of bits we had lying around. If our information was correct and the clerk was bent we were nearly in business. What I had to do was a bit complicated but if it worked we would be laughing.

Just to make sure about the shelf full of passes I toddled off to the Padre's office and asked if he would lend me a Bible as I wanted to learn more about the New Testament. He was delighted and said that if I required any help not to hesitate in going back to see him. Little did he know that I most likely knew more about the New Testament than he did, as when I was at school I had had it rammed into my thick head every day for six days a week. Strange as it may seem it was one of the subjects that I liked.

The passes were there, stacked in packs of one hundred. We offered the clerk 10 shillings (50p) for five blanks and he accepted without a murmur.

Making the light box was easy as we had all the tools and we had no problems in getting the materials. All it entailed was a plywood box with two sheets of Perspex for the lid and an electric light-bulb inside the box.

Jarvis had an old pass. I placed it between the sheets of Perspex with the blank pass fastened down with masking tape on the top; with the light switched on it was easy to see the orderly room stamp showing through the blank sheet.

It was now time for the artistic bit. With a copying pencil sharpened to a fine point I traced over the stamp, dabbed it with a damp cloth and Bob's your uncle. It was a painstaking job and took me about an hour with breaks now and again to let the bulb cool down; we later cured that problem by boring a few holes in the box.

Tubby signed the passes as Squadron Leader Bishop, which didn't matter as the Military Police who were hanging about on railway stations, or anywhere else where they could make a nuisance of themselves, didn't know the name of every commanding officer in the country.

Now that we knew that our little scam was a success it was easy to get a regular supply of blank passes from the clerk.

I took the Bible back to the Padre, thanked him for lending me it and I had made a friend for life.

We had a meeting and decided to charge three shillings (15 pence) each for the passes and everybody seemed satisfied as we had a steady trade. But as I look back on it, I think that we took a big risk for a few shillings, then again people do take risks in wartime.

One day when Group Captain Turton-Jones had been on a sortie over the North Sea, Tubby and I were in real trouble. The aircraft taxied into the dispersal and we were there to turn it round as it came slowly to a standstill. I went to put the chocks under the wheels when there was a terrific bang. It was T.J. throwing his cockpit cover back. His voice boomed out, 'Where are the bladdy armourers?' Tubby jumped up on to the wing at the side of the cockpit but all I could hear were four letter words with a court marshal or two thrown in for good measure.

By this time I had climbed up on to the wing and taken my position up behind Tubby.

What I could gather was that Group Captain Turton-Jones had been over the sea and had found himself in company with some enemy aircraft. Going by his ranting and raving it seemed that when he tried to open fire the guns had gone on strike. I had been in trouble before but this was serious.

At last, when Tubby could get a word in, he managed to ask T.J. to press the button that fired the guns, which he did, more in temper than to prove his point, and nothing happened. The button was at the top of the control column (joystick). It had a serrated edged ring round it that was the safety catch. This had to be turned in a clockwise direction before the guns would operate. Tubby leaned into the cockpit and in a quiet voice said, 'You forgot the safety catch sir.' There was no apology.

One morning the Flight Sgt came to the workshop and told us that we could have seven days' leave, going two at a time. We made him a pot of tea and off he went back to the sergeant's mess.

Tubby and I tossed a coin to see who was to go first; I lost so Tubby went first. When it came to my turn I was in two minds whether to go to Nottingham and see Alice or go home to Bradford. Nottingham won, so I got the Lincoln bus and made my way to the Nottingham road. It wasn't long before a big van pulled up. There was the driver, his mate and a soldier in the front, so there was no room for me, but the driver said that I could ride in the back as he was carrying a load of mattresses.

After a few minutes in the back on the mattresses I was fast asleep. We got to Newark and I was rudely awakened by the driver's mate telling me that I would have to get off as they were going up the Great North Road (A1). Out of curiosity I asked him where they were going and when he said Bradford I changed my mind about Alice and went home. The driver's mate gave me a funny look, slammed the tailboard up, got back into the cab and off we went.

It was the most comfortable lift I ever had and one that changed my future. It has always intrigued me how a little incident like that, or just a change of mind, can alter the rest of our lives.

I arrived home at Friday teatime and gave my mother my ration card and money. I had a quiet night in with the family and went to bed on the floor again in the front room.

The rugby season that year had gone on into the summer owing to some of the matches in the winter being postponed because of the icy weather, so on Saturday I went to Odsal Stadium to watch Bradford Northern, the local rugby team, with a pal of mine called Tom Sowden. He was a year younger than me and as yet had not gone into the forces; he did eventually join the Navy. After the match we went to Tom's house for our tea and then with his Dad to the club for a pint or two.

Tom and I arranged to go to Horton Park on Sunday night where in summer there was a band playing in the bandstand and lads and lasses congregated, more to chat each other up than listen to the band.

It was on the bridge over the duck pond that I first met Jean. There were three of them, two blonde girls and the third one with copper coloured hair and beautiful brown eyes to match; to me she was the loveliest girl that I had ever seen. Tom seemed to know them well and he walked up to them with me tagging on behind. He introduced me to Kathleen, her younger sister Doreen and the lovely Jean. At the end of the evening we walked down into Bradford with them to the tram stop and off they went to Thornbury like ships that pass in the night.

On the walk into Bradford I was troubled with my shyness and my inability to know what to talk about in female company. After a while I got chatting to the two sisters, Jean seemed on the quiet side.

I went to my bed on the dog shelf that night thinking how nice it would be to have a girlfriend like her. I soon got the thoughts out of my mind after coming to the conclusion that a girl like her must have a boyfriend somewhere.

Tom said that he would call for me at about eight o'clock on Monday night. I was wondering where we would go for a pint or two, when he turned up with a brown paper parcel under his arm. He had arranged to see Kathleen at 'Bert Shutts', the local dance hall and took it for granted that I would be going with him. Not wanting to spoil his night I joined him, thinking if the worst came to the worst I could always take refuge in the Red Lion pub next door, after all, while dancing with Alice at the Miners' Welfare it hadn't taken me long to discover that I had two left feet.

We paid our money at the door and went in; inside were Kathleen and the lovely Jean waiting for us. Tom got Kathleen up to dance and there I was all on my own with Jean. I couldn't ask her to dance as I didn't know how. I felt silly just stood there, not knowing what to say, when she asked me if I would like to dance; I felt sillier still when I told her that I couldn't dance, but she replied that she wasn't that good herself but would try and teach me if I wanted.

It was a waltz and, following a struggle with her teaching me the basic steps, I felt that I was on cloud nine. Her saying that she wasn't so good was what you could call being a stranger to the truth. I didn't get to the Red Lion after all.

At the end of the night we walked with them to the trolley bus that would get them near their homes. In those days, even in the blackout, girls could go about at night feeling safe. Before getting on the bus Jean mentioned that she would be there again on Wednesday night if I fancied carrying on with my dancing lessons. I couldn't believe what I was hearing and it seemed ages before Wednesday night came along. I think I was falling in love.

On the Wednesday night she was by herself, so after the dancing I asked her if I could go on the bus with her and see her home. Her home was at the top end of Woodhall Road at Thornbury and we stood chatting by the unlit lamp outside the house for a while. I plucked up courage to give her a kiss and a cuddle and all went well. It was like that in those days, well, it was for me anyway. In these more promiscuous days it would be 'Your place or mine?' and straight into bed.

I was due back off leave on Friday but Tubby had volunteered to stand in for me on the Saturday and Sunday and to sign one of our passes for me, so Saturday was the last day of my leave, as I would be hitch-hiking back on the Sunday. Jean and I went to the cinema at Stanningley on Saturday night.

We had only been standing outside her house for a couple of minutes after me walking her home when the door opened and a chap on the step said, 'You may as well come in.'

It was George, Jean's dad. After being introduced to George and Lillie it was tea and biscuits then mother and dad went to bed so we had our kiss and cuddle in comfort. It was a good two miles walk back to Royd Street but it didn't seem two hundred yards. It was the beginning of a long romance and broken hearts.

My journey back to Digby wasn't as good as the one from Digby to Bradford; no mattresses this time. I hitched a lift to Wakefield, then to Doncaster and an RAF wagon all the way to Lincoln.

Now that I had something to go to Bradford for it didn't take long for me to talk Tubby into a scheme by which we could do 48 hours on and 48 hours off and sometimes we could extend it to 72 hours. So with the forged leave passes and making sure that we were back every other Friday for pay parade, everything in the garden smelt of roses.

The risks that we were taking didn't seem to bother us at the time even though we only needed one sneaky prat to grass on us and our rose garden would have turned into weeds.

I was managing to get to Bradford about once a fortnight. Jean was writing to me almost every other day and her letters were getting more romantic all the time.

Towards the end of August I was called back to Watnall, which goes to prove that all good things come to an end, so it was back to the gun pits and sentry boxes.

On arriving at Watnall they told me there was no room for me on the camp and I would be billeted out. I got fixed up in a house on a little housing estate below the village with a Mr and Mrs Plant so it meant that I did one night on guard and the next night with home comforts. Mr Plant worked at a coalmine nearby where he worked shifts of two weeks on days and two weeks on nights. He was a nice chap and when he was on days and it was my night off we would go to a pub at the top of the village called the Queens Head. He always insisted on buying me my beer as miners had at last started getting a decent wage.

It got to October and the nights were getting colder. One night, when her husband was on the night shift, Mrs Plant, as bold as brass, said that if it was cold in the little bedroom I could sleep with her in her bed. She was twenty-eight, which seemed old to me at the time, and another thing was that I wouldn't be able to look her husband in the face again. On reflection I think if it hadn't been for Jean I would have been tempted. As I was still a cock virgin it may have been a good way to be introduced to the carnal pleasures but I didn't take up the offer.

A few nights later, when I was on guard duty, Alice came to Mrs Plant's looking for me. One of my pals had seen her at the Miners' Welfare and told her that I was back at Watnall and where I was billeted. The next day Mrs Plant went up to the camp and told the adjutant that she wasn't going to put up with girls coming looking for me every night of the week. I was living back in the camp the following day.

I had only been back in the camp a few days when the corporal taking the morning parade turned up with a clipboard and some sheets of paper on it which was never a good sign. The general gist of the papers was that the people who sat around in London had decided to make the Ground Gunners into the RAF Regiment or Ground Observers. It was a case of you, you and you again and, yet again, we weren't given a choice.

In my innocence I didn't notice that the lads selected to go on the Observers' Course to St. Athan in South Wales had all done detention or jankers (service slang for confined to camp) at some time. I had been selected to go on the Observers' Course.

I had visions of being in a comfy little lookout post on the east coast watching out for German aircraft coming to bomb inland from me. Like the fellow that gets married a second time, I was a born optimist.

In two days' time we were off to 'Taffy Land' on the train from

Nottingham to Gloucester where we had to have a two hour wait and then proceed to Cardiff. There was a chap with us called Priest who I noticed had another parcel with him besides his own kitbag and backpack. As the train pulled out of the station I asked him casually what he had in his parcel. His answer was that it was a radio that he had pinched out the NAAFI at Watnall the night before. All our criminal minds working in unison said, 'You silly bugger.' We had to explain to him that when we got to St. Athan they would have telephoned through from Watnall to search us as we reported in at the guardroom. He didn't pass the Observers' Course – lucky for him. Some bright spark came up with the idea that we would have to sell it in a second hand shop in Gloucester when we changed trains. Someone else suggested that we throw it out of the carriage window. I thought that was the best idea but Priest wanted a few bob for going to the risk and trouble of breaking and entering to get it so a secondhand deal it was. I was chosen to go with him as we didn't think that Priest was bright enough to do the haggling with the dealer.

After all this palaver it happened to be half-day closing when we finally arrived at Gloucester. The only shop we could find open was a charity shop where it was gratefully received.

We arrived at St. Athan about 10pm and reported in at the guards' room sited at the entrance to the camp and manned by the service police. In the dark, sat with his back to us, was a sergeant. I told him that we were on the Ground Observers' Course and that we had come to sign in. Without turning around he said, 'Hello Dave, how are you?' It was my old friend Corporal Bell who had been so kind to me when I did my detention at Watnall. He had recognised my broad Yorkshire accent. This was an excuse to be apart from the other lads and I pretended to catch up on old times with him. What I really wanted was to tell him that I had five more days' jankers to do carried over from Watnall. He told me to forget about it.

So this was St. Athan. Its claim to fame was at the time that it was the biggest RAF station in the land.

A police corporal took us to our billet for the next few weeks. It was a big hangar with about three hundred beds all lined up in rows like soldiers on parade.

It was more than cold and my bed was at the end of a row next to one of the hangar doors. On the third day there it was the same hangar door that got me into trouble. It was six o'clock in the morning and I was bursting for a piss. I got out of my bed, slid the hangar door back and relieved myself. I was fastening my fly hole (it was so cold that we slept in our trousers) when a voice behind me said, 'You're on a charge.' It was a snotty-nosed corporal. What he was doing snooping about at that time of the morning I don't know. Maybe he was on his way back to his quarters after a night in the WAAF's compound and in a bad mood because he didn't get his end away.

The charge was 'urinating against the hangar door at 06.00 hours.' Seven days confined to camp. It wasn't the confined to camp bit that troubled me as there was nowhere to go outside the camp at night, it was the three hours peeling spuds every night behind the cookhouse in the freezing cold.

Every two or three days I wrote to Jean and I kept on receiving letters from her; she was writing to me so often that she must have been finding it difficult to think of what to write about as she had started putting the words of popular love songs in her letters to fill the pages.

After the Observers' Course had been going a week or so, I got a bit suspicious. Firstly they told us that we wouldn't be having any training in small arms as we already had plenty of experience in that field, so at first it was naturally aircraft recognition. Then other lessons started creeping into the course, like how to find your own water and what types of animals and other things were fit to eat if we ever got desperate. Every few days they took us down to the coast to a place called Porthcawl for lessons in seamanship on an air-sea rescue launch. Then there was map reading and how to give weather reports. It looked like I could forget about that nice little observation post on the east coast.

After six weeks, as the course was nearing an end, we were in the gym having lessons in unarmed combat from a sergeant PTI (physical training instructor) who had a face like a pig and tattoos on his arms. 'Now then, you lot, I am going to demonstrate what would happen if you was confronted by a German soldier.' I knew what would happen if I was confronted by anyone that wanted to kill me; I would be on my bike in double quick time.

Why he picked on me as his first victim I will never know but he did. 'Come out here you.' He was on a mat so that when he threw me up in the air, in theory I would land on the mat and not get hurt. 'Right lad, I want you to hit me under the chin.' I had done all this before in my primary training so I knew what was going to happen. He would, quick as a flash, grab my wrist as my fist travelled towards his chin, twist me round and push my arm up my back. So with me being a clever bugger and not having the sense to think of the future I didn't strike at his chin, instead I sidestepped to his right, went in around his waist and slid down to his legs. It was the perfect rugby tackle and he went down like a ton of bricks; he was much bigger than me but on reflection everyone I had played rugby against was bigger than me.

We got to our feet and at first words failed him; he was red in the face and his fists were clenched; what made it worse was that all the other silly sods were laughing. I was already seeing the stars before my eyes. At that moment our section officer walked into the gym with a clipboard under his arm. Talk about being saved by the bell.

We all sprang to attention, including the sergeant; the officer told us to stand easy. The sergeant was standing behind him making aggressive gestures in my direction which I read as meaning he was going to tear me into little bits and push the bits up my Khyber Pass.

The section officer began his speech by saying that he had good news for some trainees and not so good for others. He would start off by calling out the names of the ones that had passed. The ones that he didn't call out had failed.

I passed, but in the years that followed I never got round to figuring out whether the good news was for the ones that had passed or the ones that had failed. He went on to say that the ones that had passed with high marks would be promoted to LAC (Leading Aircraftsman). I was now an LAC.

The ones that had passed would be leaving for White Waltham within the next twenty-four hours. We would be issued with tropical kit. We were to be given seven days' embarkation leave. It was like receiving a prison sentence, except for the leave.

We arrived at White Waltham and were shown into a Nissen hut where we were to be billeted for the next week or so.

After getting ourselves sorted out we got talking to the lads that had been there a few days and found that some of them were wireless operators. Others were drivers and the rest consisted of clerks, store bashers etc., and we were to be formed into a unit that would be known as 23 WOU (Wireless Observer Unit).

After we had been there a day or two we were taken to a place called West Drayton where they issued us with our tropical kit.

The bit that amused us most was the hat or topi; it was the same type I had seen in a film about Kitchener's army at the battle of Khartoum. It made us wonder where they had stored them away for sixty years or so.

One bright spark said a pal of his had been issued with tropical kit and finished up in Iceland.

The next day we were given leave and off I went to Bradford.

It was the middle of December and had turned cold with a bit of snow on the ground.

Jean was pleased to see me but not so pleased when I told her it would be the last time we would be together for a long time, maybe for years.

I was wrong, for when we got back to White Waltham they told us we could go home for Christmas.

It was the loveliest Christmas I had ever had. I took Jean to see my parents and we went for tea to her grandma's a couple of times. She was a lovely old lady; her husband had been killed in the First World War.

The day after Jean had met my parents my dad gave me a bit of fatherly advice by saying, 'She is a grand girl so don't go and do something which you will be sorry for after.' As I knew I would be going away for a long time I had reluctantly made my mind up regarding his advice before he had given it to me, although at the time we found it hard to do.

Following the New Year the unit moved to West Kirby, where I had done my primary training. The troopship at Liverpool was getting nearer all the time.

After being there a few days I decided to sneak off to Bradford, as nothing seemed to be happening. I stayed for about four days before deciding it was time I showed my face at West Kirby again.

George (Jean's dad) had a job driving a petrol tanker that he picked up at 11 o'clock at night from a depot in Bradford and took to Trafford Park near Manchester to be filled up, and then drove back to Bradford. I got a lift with him as far as the East Lancs Road.

I hadn't been walking for long when a little greengrocery

wagon stopped and picked me up. It was bitterly cold and I had to ride on the back as he had his mate in the front with him, so I was open to the elements. The good bit was that he was going all the way to Liverpool.

All I know about the rest of the journey is going through the Mersey Tunnel.

It was still dark when I got to the hole in the fence that was only about twenty yards from the door of our hut.

It was pitch dark inside and the light switch was at the other end of the hut, I was groping my way down the centre of the room, when there was a loud bang and I saw stars and blinding lights. I had bumped into the stove in the middle of the room and banged my head on the stove pipe. Besides giving me a bit of a shock my head was bleeding.

The shock was nothing like the shock I got when I switched the lights on.

The place was empty: they had gone on the ship.

What could I do now?

As we were an independent unit we had not had any contact with anyone else on the camp. I thought that the only thing I could do was go to the orderly room and hope someone there would be able to sort things out.

There was one thing for certain. I would be in serious trouble and be put on a charge, which more than likely would finish up with a court martial.

The only person in the orderly room was a flight sergeant who said that he was 'half expecting' me to turn up, that is if I turned up at all.

He seemed a decent sort and gave me some advice on what I should say to the commanding officer when I was up in front of him at 9.30am.

It went something like this; 'Don't tell him that you went to Bradford as that would be the first offence as Bradford is out of bounds. Tell him that you went to Chester, which is in bounds, and that you got drunk with two civilians. Say you were sick all down the front of your uniform and that you fell on your head. One of them took you to his house and put you on the settee and his wife put your uniform into soak and washed it next morning, it took all day to dry and that is why you didn't get back to camp until last night, Sir.'

How he had thought all this up on the spur of the moment I don't know. He also told me that the CO always asked him what punishment he should dole out, he said that he would suggest 14 days confined to camp. He must have been feeling really sorry for me.

At 9.15 I had my cap knocked off and was marched into the CO's office.

When I saw his face it struck me immediately that the flight sergeant had been pulling my leg.

The CO had a face like a pig, and a sadistic pig to boot, the only bit of hope I could get from his face was he looked like a heavy drinker.

After reading the charges out to me and telling me about the seriousness of missing a ship he asked me if I would accept his punishment or request a court martial. I couldn't believe my ears.

I answered promptly that I would accept his punishment.

He gave me 14 days confined to camp, I was beginning to realise that there were some nice people in the RAF after all, even officers with piggy faces.

When doing jankers you had to go on parade each night to be inspected by the orderly officer and to make sure that you were still there. This was after you had done a few hours spud bashing (peeling potatoes) or cleaning latrines in the officers' quarters etc.

One night on parade I heard the officer giving one of the lads a bollocking for having dirty buttons on his greatcoat. When I heard the lad's reply I recognised the voice of my old pal Austin Bergan. It was the first time we'd met since joining up together. He was doing 7 days for being sick on a sergeant on a bus in Southport.

He had been stationed at Formby and still had 3 days' jankers to do at West Kirby. I also had another 3 days to go.

When we finished our punishments we had a good night out in Hoylake (drunk again).

Austin was now in the RAF Regiment and was off to Liverpool next day to board a troopship. I didn't see him again for over three years.

After a few more days at West Kirby I was back again at White Waltham where another new unit was being formed and was to be known as 24 WOU.

There was a lad called Wilson who had been there the last time same as I had. He had gone one better than me and when the ship had pulled out into the river to form up into a convoy, he had jumped off and swum to New Brighton where he was picked up on the beach by the police.

Same as me he had only got 14 days. It wasn't long before we found why they had been so lenient with us, as anyone who had the misfortune to have travelled on a troopship in those days will tell you.

We were at White Waltham for another week or two and nothing seemed to be happening, we even got another 7 days embarkation leave.

My parents and Jean must have started wondering if I was kidding about going abroad.

It was another seven days that passed on too quickly, like they do when you are with someone you are madly in love with.

A day or two after the leave we moved from White Waltham to Cosford near Wolverhampton. When we had been at Cosford a few days nothing seemed to be happening so I decided to slope off home again for a day or two.

How I had the nerve to do this after what happened to me the first time beats me as these days it takes a lot of nerve for me to cross a road. Perhaps it was what they call the folly of youth or maybe it was that love knows no bounds.

I left one and sixpence with a pal of mine called Ginger Speakman and asked him to send me a telegram if it looked like something was happening before I got back.

I got a lift to Manchester on the back of a wagon again. Getting off the wagon I fell to the floor, my legs had frozen. Two old men picked me up and rubbed my legs to get the circulation going again. One of them kept rambling on about how it used to happen to them in the trenches in the First World War.

These things never seem to happen to the people who create these wars in order to line their own pockets.

When I got to Manchester station I had a bit of luck as there was a train leaving for Bradford from platform 13 in about five minutes.

I got my ticket and was making my way to the platform when I noticed from the corner of my eye two red caps who were watching me out of the corners of their eyes.

I strolled casually behind the bookstall, keeping it between the red caps and me until I got through the ticket barrier and on to the platform.

As I opened the carriage door I glanced back and saw them coming through the ticket barrier, they looked like a couple of bloodhounds who I had once seen in the film 'Convict 99'.

Not being sure which carriage I had got into I could hear them coming along the platform opening and closing the carriage doors. It was time to get my thinking cap on.

The compartments in those days were all separate from each other unless it was a corridor train which fortunately for me this one wasn't. So I was out of the door at the other side of the compartment intending to escape that way but my luck was in again. When I opened the door I saw that there was a wooden step and two big brass handholds, one on each side of the door. So with the door closed and standing on the wooden step holding on to the handles and crouching down I couldn't be seen.

Just as the train was pulling out I heard them open and close the other door and move on. I was on my way to Bradford once again but thought that when they found out that they had been tricked they could ring through to Bradford station. So I got off in the pitch dark at St. Dunstan's which was the last stop before Bradford. I jumped over the railings and was on my way rejoicing.

After three days at home I was beginning to get the wind up as there had been no telegram from Ginger so I decided to high-tail it back to Cosford.

On the last night with Jean I was sorely tempted to go the whole way with our emotions. Whether it was self discipline or the old guilt complex or that I was scared of the consequences I will never know. On arriving back at Cosford it was a relief to find that nothing was happening. I told Ginger to keep the one and sixpence.

The morning after arriving back at Cosford we were on parade and the flight sergeant called the roll as usual, my name wasn't called, he scratched his head and said, 'Usually we are one or two short, today we have one too many. Whose name hasn't been called?' I put my hand up, he put my name on his list and asked me if I had got a rifle, which I hadn't. He then took me to the stores where I signed for one and that was it.

That night a few of us went down into Wolverhampton.

Wilson, the lad who had jumped the last ship, was with us. We got settled down for the night in a cosy little pub with a nice fire going.

Wilson kept going on about ways he could dodge going on the next ship. His opportunity came walking into the pub about five minutes before closing time in the shape of a police sergeant and constable. After they had had their walk around and were on their way out, Wilson went into action. He blocked their way and told them that they were out and out prats and that they had been conceived by parents who weren't married.

The sergeant reprimanded him and told him to behave himself.

I noticed that Wilson's gas mask bag with his tin hat on it was dangling at his side. Up it came in one swift movement and struck the sergeant on the side of his head. That was the final straw, out came the handcuffs and off went Wilson calling out to us in a jubilant tone of voice that he would be on a civvy charge and he wouldn't be joining us poor sods on the ship.

When we got back to camp at about 11.30pm we were glad to get into our pits (beds) with our bellies full of beer but frozen stiff.

After having our usual moan about things in general and chat about home, like all servicemen seem to do at bedtime, the door opened and in came the flight sergeant along with a flurry of snow.

'Right lads, out of your pits and get packed, reveille at six-thirty, breakfast at seven and on our way at eight,' and off he went.

4
The Troopship

There we were, all lined up on Gladstone Dock at Liverpool. In front of us was a big ship. It was called *The Duchess of Richmond* but I found out later that you don't call ships 'it', you always address them as 'she'.

She was the first ship I had ever seen, apart from the ones on films, and the size of her made my mind boggle. I found out later that she weighed twenty-eight thousand tons and belonged to the Canadian Pacific Line. All the Canadian Pacific boats had flat bottoms to enable them to get up the Hudson River in Canada, which I am told is very shallow in parts. They were all named after some Duchess or other and were known as the 'Drunken Duchesses' owing to their antics in a rough sea

We waited three hours on Gladstone Dock before starting boarding. Whilst we were waiting along came Wilson handcuffed to a brace of red caps. They took him straight up the gangplank and banged him into the only cell on the ship. He was in that cell for eight weeks and he was the only member of the other ranks to have a bunk.

At the end of the three hours we started boarding and were taken down to E deck, which was just above the water line so it had port holes which hadn't to be opened at sea in case the Atlantic Ocean popped in.

She had been a cruise ship before the war, but now she had been converted into a troopship to carry 2,000 men. She was presently carrying 4,000 as the war was getting a bit out of control and we seemed to be losing at every turn.

Anyone who has not been on a troopship at that time cannot possibly imagine what it was like; they were very much like the slave ships of the 1700s.

Every compartment between the bulkheads had been cleared. From the sides of the ship there were tables about three feet apart with two forms, one for each table in the three foot space. Each table seated sixteen men; above the tables were hooks for the hammocks. When the hammocks were slung they were all touching, so that if a man wanted to get out of his hammock the one at the end had to get out first and the others follow on.

Two men slept on each table and two under the table. I was lucky enough to get my space under the table with my head to the side of the ship.

At meal times there were two sittings and I was on the second sitting so that the first sitting at breakfast had their feet on me. When it came to the second sitting all I had to do was to crawl out into my space at the table and have my porridge and bread roll.

We slept in our clothes in case we got torpedoed. It was known as 'sleeping all standing' but whatever that has got to do with sleeping with our clothes on I'll never know. Between the tables and the companionway leading to the deck above was open space but at night it was covered with bodies. This all seemed a bit rough but it could have been much worse as there was a battalion of the Black Watch Regiment sleeping out on the open decks.

On Thursday afternoon all the ships started moving out of the docks and into the middle of the river, we thought that we were off but, no.

German bombers came that night and bombed the whole seven mile length of the docks; the overhead railway, which ran the full length of the docks, didn't exist anymore.

Maybe a British spy in Germany had found out about the raid and let his or her counterpart in England know about it in the nick of time.

The next morning was Friday the 13th.

All the ships started moving slowly out of the river and forming into a convoy.

I was leaning on the rail watching the Liver Building fading into the gloom; next to me leaning on the rail was a soldier of the Green Howard's Regiment. He was much older than me and tears were trickling down his cheeks. I didn't know what to say, which was unusual for me. After a while he said, 'That's the last time we will see that building and last week was the last time I'll have seen my wife and two kids.' He came from Keighley and I often wondered afterwards if he ever did get back. There would be plenty of men on that ship that didn't.

I had already made my mind up that if I didn't get back it would be no fault of mine. Self preservation and survival were to be my motto and to hope for a land for heroes to live in if there were any left. All I could think of was getting home to Jean.

It wasn't long before I palled up with a couple of lads on the same mess table as me. We got talking, like you do, about sport and I mentioned that I had played a bit of junior rugby. They had both been professional boxers and we became pals for a long time. Frank Routledge was from Liverpool and was a born comedian like most Scousers. Bill Connor was a more serious type and came from Preston. They were both drivers on the same unit as me. Bill had been stationed at Kirkham near Blackpool, which had been handy for him to get home to Preston. While he was at Preston he fell foul of a sergeant who also came from Preston. One morning the sergeant came into the transport section with a list of half a dozen names who were to be posted overseas. Bill was at the top of his list.

Bill's wife Peg was four months pregnant and when her nine months was up she gave birth to a girl. It was to be four years before he saw her, for when I came home after nearly three years he was posted to the Far East.

Sometimes he used to rehearse what he was going to do to the sergeant when he caught up with him after the war; it wasn't very pleasant.

Frank came from a family of ten brothers and one sister, so he knew a bit about survival and being hungry and how being hungry made you fight when you got into the boxing ring.

When we got clear of the Mersey and into the Irish Sea the convoy turned north which seemed a bit strange. It became clearer after a while when a lot more ships joined the convoy off the entrance to the Clyde. We found out later that it was the biggest convoy to leave Britain in the whole of the war so far.

We turned north past a great big rock that one of the more worldly-wise types said was 'Paddy's milestone'.

Off the north-east corner of Northern Ireland there was a lot of hooting going on from all the ships' sirens and we were heading west into the North Atlantic.

All this I learned from lads like Frank, as my knowledge of geography at the time was nil.

After we got well out into the Atlantic and turned south the sea got very rough. This was a stroke of luck in some ways as the U-boats were unable to operate in a sea so rough.

The clever fellow that told us this was then violently sick over the rail and that was the start of the 'mal de mer'.

After we had had our tiffin (lunch), an army officer came down to the mess deck with his clipboard at the ready.

'Right, you chaps, I have here a list of twenty-four names and I have been informed that these men have been trained as machine gunners.' I thought 'here it comes'. I was top of the list again.

While the ship had been in dock at Liverpool the shore workers had built two gun turrets on a raised up deck aft of the anchor deck and forward of the well deck to the front of the bridge.

He took us up to the turrets and explained to us that we would be split up into two parties of six doing twenty-four hours on and twenty-four off. When we were on we were to team up in twos doing two hours on and four off and we would be excused mess duties.

I had heard a lot of talk about seasickness and imagined that I would be one of the first to suffer; I was wrong, as the bouncing about didn't affect me.

Bill Connor and I were the only two that turned up for breakfast on Sunday morning. On Sundays it was a special treat; porridge, a hard boiled egg, a little brown bun loaf and a mug of tea. On the other six days we didn't get the egg.

There were sixteen of us on the table, so Bill and I had a dixie of porridge, sixteen hard boiled eggs and the bun loaves to go at. I managed two plates of porridge, four eggs and three loaves. Bill managed a lot more than me as he was a much bigger lad.

That night the sea got worse, the lads who were sleeping on the deck between the tables and the stairs were lying in vomit, the stink was horrible.

After a while things began to settle down and develop a kind of routine. I found that the duty on the gun turret wasn't so bad after all as it helped to ease the boredom.

The weather was getting a little warmer each day as we headed south.

On some evenings Frank, Bill and an Irish lad called Paddy Boyce made a habit of sitting on a life raft on the open deck for an hour or so. Paddy was also a boxer so the conversation was usually about boxing and I just had to listen. I found out that there is much more about the noble art than climbing into the ring and knocking hell out of each other. It had more to do with managers, agents and money.

One day when I had finished my two hour shift on the guns I got talking to a couple of deckhands who were painting the turrets with red lead. Having been a painter what seemed a hundred years ago, I stood watching them for a while and one of them said jokingly, 'Do you want to have a go mate?' To join in the joke I said 'Give me your brush.' which he did and I got to slapping it on in fine style. The two of them stood watching and having a smoke. I had no sooner started enjoying myself when the Bosun appeared (the deckhands' boss). The two deckhands looked a bit sheepish when he wanted to know what was going on. They told him that I had been a painter in civvy street and I was keeping my hand in. He studied for a moment or two and said, 'If you want to keep your hand in I'm always short of willing hands.' Without thinking, I broke the golden rule and volunteered.

He took me to the Bosun's locker (store) and fixed me up with a scraper, a chipping hammer, paint can, brush and best of all a boiler suit with the Canadian Pacific crest on the front.

There is always plenty of painting to do on a ship, so along I went in my spare time with Ginger and Taffy painting and learning the names of the different parts of the ship. After a day or two they took me down to their mess deck at break time where there was always a good pot of tea and jam and bread.

The days were getting warmer now and I was beginning to think that life at sea wasn't so bad after all. There were still some things that were not so good; like the weevils in our little brown bun loaves. Before we ate them we knocked them on the table and the weevils fell out and ran away.

After a while we didn't bother knocking them out; we must have been getting short of meat in our diet. It just goes to show that nature has its way of showing us what we need.

Another problem was the latrines. They had been built on the open decks with timber and plywood; on the inside there was a step that ran the full length of the latrine. About eighteen inches up from the step was a plank with about ten holes in it. The holes were just about big enough to fit a medium sized arse.

Underneath the plank was a trough with a slight slope from one end to the other; seawater was pumped in at the top end taking everything in its path with it out of the hole at the bottom end and into the sea.

A fantastic piece of plumbing most likely designed by some boffin sat in a comfy office in London.

There is always a snag and the snag was that sometimes the outlet hole at the bottom end of the plank would get blocked up. So the men sat on the plank would have the discomfort of the contents of the trough lapping up against their bare arses and private parts.

A big stick was provided in order to clear the hole when it got blocked up. There could be ten men on the plank all shouting in chorus. 'For fuck's sake, clear the hole!' to the lad at the end with the stick.

You may have noticed by now if you have had the time or patience to read this chronicle, or whatever you would like to call it, that up to now I have tried not to use any four letter words. The simple reason is that four letter words were used to such an extent in the forces that this story would be twice as long if they were included.

The further south we went the warmer the weather got. The fresh water tanks were getting lower so the order came that the other ranks were to be rationed. They were to have their water bottles filled at the galley 'cookhouse' each morning and that was to last them until the following morning. I can't remember just how much our bottles held, it may have been one and a half pints and that had to do for drinking and our tea.

It was said at the time that the officers were still having fresh water showers.

After we had filled our bottles we stacked them at the top end of the mess table with our name and number written on them in indelible pencil.

I was lucky working with Ginger and Taffy as I could always nip down to the crews' mess and get a drink.

One afternoon we were caulking a lifeboat and Taffy asked me if I had anything to read. I hadn't but Paddy had just finished a book called *The Gun* by C. S. Forester and I said that I would go and ask him for a lend of it.

I found Paddy and off we went down to the mess deck to get the book out of his small kit. When we got to the bottom of the companionway (stairs) there was no one about as all the lads were up on deck sunning themselves. It seemed dark down there after the bright sunlight but when my eyes began to focus properly I saw a Glasgow hard man called Crawford drinking water out of a bottle with the name Evans on it. I didn't know what to do, as Crawford was much bigger than the pair of us and nasty with it too.

Before I knew what was happening Paddy went up to him saying, 'That isn't your water.'

Crawford replied, 'And what are you going to do about it you Irish duck egg?'

Never before have I ever seen anything so quick, Paddy took a step backwards then there was a crack like someone breaking a piece of wood.

Crawford crumpled up into an untidy heap on the deck, out for the count. We dragged the unconscious body along to the sick bay, knocked on the door and scarpered.

When Crawford appeared on the mess deck a day or two later we learned that he had a broken jaw; it kept him quiet for a long time.

Taffy got his book, Paddy got two broken fingers and I found out why boxers wear gloves.

It was a lovely night, there was a warm breeze being made by the forward motion of the ship, the sea was calm and inky black. There was no moon, which made the stars look like diamonds in the sky and reflected in the calm sea.

Bill and I were leaning on the rail watching the phosphorescence sparkling in the wash from the side of the ship, we were both lost in our thoughts. I expect Bill was thinking about Peg and the baby and I was thinking about the lovely Jean.

Bill had been a bit worried lately as he hadn't had a bowel movement since eating the ten hard-boiled eggs when we were off the west coast of Ireland.

There we were at peace with the world when suddenly Bill said in a calm tone of voice, 'I've shit!' He didn't have to tell me. It was horrible. Thankfully, he had shorts on and there it was running down his legs and into the scuppers like lava erupting from a volcano.

At St. Athan, on our course, they had given us a few lessons on first aid telling us how to make splints for broken bones and how to apply a tourniquet etc., but never for anything like this. My dad used to tell me that necessity is the mother of invention and this was the necessity bit.

Just nearby was a hosepipe on a reel that the crew used for washing the decks down in the mornings, I dashed over to the reel and unwound a length of hose, turned on the valve and presto, I was in business, but not as much business as poor old Bill was in.

A sergeant who was leaning on the rail nearby came over and was going to give me a bollocking for playing with the hosepipe but changed his mind when he saw what I was doing, he just held his nose and walked away.

A few mornings after Bill's big shit I was rudely awakened by a loud clanking noise, the whole of the ship seemed to be vibrating. There I was on my bed space under the table as usual with my head on my life-jacket, at first I thought that we had run aground on some rocks. It didn't take long for me to figure out what was happening when I remembered that for the last day or two a couple of the crew had been servicing the anchor winches. That was it, we were hooked on to old mother earth at last.

There weren't many lads about on the mess deck and I could only see about half a dozen pairs of feet of the first sitting from my viewpoint under the table.

The first lad that I saw was Harry Clark a wireless operator, he came from Stockton Heath near Warrington, later on he became a good pal. The type that would stick by you through thick and thin. He said, 'Look out of the porthole,' so I climbed up on to the table, looked out of the porthole and there it was before my very eyes: Africa!

5
Africa

The first thing that crossed my mind was the geography teacher at school describing what I could now see before me.

There were a few more ships at anchor in the bay and two Sunderland flying boats that looked much bigger than I had imagined.

Surrounding the bay was a sandy beach with the hillsides behind it covered in trees. Nestled in the middle of all this and coming right down to the beach was a small town. It was Freetown, the capital of Sierra Leone, West Africa, otherwise known as the 'White Man's Grave' because of the cholera and other diseases that were rife along that coast.

It wasn't long before lots of small boats, known as bumboats, were coming out to the ship from the beaches. When they got close to the ship we saw that they were laden down to the gunnels with bananas. What then followed was that the natives on the boat threw a line up to us on the ship. On the end of the line was a basket that you hoisted up, put a sixpence (or 'tanner' as we called them) in the basket, lowered it down and pulled it up again with ten bananas in it. In those days there was a coin smaller in size than a sixpence called a threepenny bit. Now and again one of the lads would put one of these coins in the basket, when the basket reached the boat they would shout, 'Glasgow tanners, no good', it was a waste of time trying to trick these Freetown lads.

When there was a bit of a lull in the banana business they would sing a song for us, the first line went 'Queen Victoria is a very good man.' I can't remember how the rest of it went but it made us laugh. I seem to remember it being a bit smutty.

We were anchored in the bay at Freetown for over a week filling up with water and refuelling etc.

Where to next?

We were off again and the weather was getting warmer still as the convoy trailed its way on towards the equator. The number of ships in the convoy was much smaller as a number of them had left us at Gibraltar and gone into the Mediterranean. Sadly for many of them never to return.

One night there was a tropical thunderstorm, which is a fantastic sight at sea.

We then had the crossing of the line ceremony when we were given a certificate making us subjects of King Neptune.

Each day as we headed south the North Star became the Southern Cross and if we had had plugholes we would have noticed that the water swirled the other way round going down the hole. I have never had it explained to me why this happens, maybe one day some clever fellow will tell me.

After heading south for what seemed a good many days we turned east to round the Cape of Good Hope where I saw my first whale. At first I thought it was a small island until it suddenly started spouting water.

The weather had turned and no wonder, for when I mentioned to Taffy and Ginger, the two crew men, they told me that the nearest land to the south was the Antarctic. I was learning more geography every day.

A day or two later we changed course to the northeast which took us up the east coast of South Africa. We always seemed to make our landfalls in the morning and this bright and sunny morning revealed Durban in all its glory.

What a sight it was for a lad from the back streets of Bradford. A promenade lined with palm trees, the beautiful buildings, against a backdrop of hills with bungalows set here and there amongst the orange groves.

The docks at Durban are in a kind of a lagoon, there is a piece of land that comes out from the shore about a mile from the entrance. It goes out about one hundred yards then turns to run parallel with the shore and back to the entrance. The docks are on the landward side. All this makes it a natural harbour and well sheltered from the heavy surf that drives in from the Indian Ocean.

On entering the docks I noticed that on our starboard side we were looking down on to a prison with a high wall around it. There was a big compound surrounded by cell blocks. In the compound were dozens of men dressed in blue and white striped overalls working on some task or other. They were all Blacks and they were all manacled. It just goes to show that all that glitters is not gold. Not for some, anyway.

No sooner had the crew got the ship tied up than there appeared on the dockside a lady with a megaphone. She sang songs that were popular at the time to us who by now were lining the rails to listen to her. She had a lovely voice and it was said that she entertained the troops on every ship that docked at Durban and at that time there were a lot of ships. The lady was dressed all in white and because of this was known by troops from all over the world as the Lady in White.

A rumour was going round the ship that we were being allowed ashore at 12·30. A lad called Crowley and I were unlucky because at 12·30 everybody was trooping ashore and being picked up by civilians with cars waiting to take lads to their houses to be wined, dined and entertained.

With Crowley and me being on the gun turrets earlier in the voyage we had been excused mess duty but now we weren't needed on the guns we had to do mess duties like everyone else and that day it happened to be our turn. With it being 'tiffin time' we were left with a pile of plates and mess tins to wash so that when we finally got ashore all the civilians and cars had gone.

After getting off the ship and out of the dock gates we made our way towards the town; it seemed strange to be on dry land again. We decided to take a short cut and finished up about a mile inland where the houses were more working-class. After a while we came to an open space of scrubland.

I couldn't believe my eyes at what I saw across the wasteland. It was the shanty town where the majority of the blacks lived or to use a better word existed. The houses were just corrugated iron shelters with what looked like pieces of sacking for the doors; the sanitation must have been terrible judging by the stench that was drifting towards us on the breeze.

The whole set-up made our back-to-back houses in Bradford

look like palaces. It just goes to show that somewhere in the world there is always someone worse off than you: Like the man with no boots said when he met the man with no feet.

After getting our sense of direction sorted we set off in the direction of the town.

Just by where we were was a small general store so as we were feeling a bit peckish we went in for something to eat. The first things to meet my eyes were dozens of bars of chocolate, I couldn't believe it, as chocolate in England had been in short supply for quite a while. We got a couple of bars each hoping that it wouldn't melt before we could eat it as the weather was on the warm side.

There was a little coloured boy about seven or eight years old before us in the shop. He got half a loaf of bread and asked the shopkeeper to put it in the book, which meant that his mother would pay for it at the end of the week. This was nothing new to me as it was common practice where I lived when I was young but I never remember my mother sending me for a half loaf of bread.

We carried on our way eating our chocolate when my mate Crowley said, 'Why didn't we buy the boy some chocolate?'

Why is it that we always think of what we should have done when it's too late? I didn't enjoy the second bar.

When we got back to the centre of the town, where all the lovely buildings were, we met some army lads who told us that a hundred yards or so down the road was a Catholic Club where we could get free food. Off we went and true enough there was the club. It was up some stairs on the first floor. It always amazes me how servicemen have a way of finding these places as there were quite a few in.

A lady came up to us and asked us to sign the book stating name, hometown and religion. I put Roman Catholic, nudging Crowley to do the same; I thought that it might get us a better helping. They served us a lovely piece of steak with chips, fried onions, mushrooms and side salad finished off with a lovely pot of tea. We couldn't have had a better feed in the 'Savoy Hotel', not that I have ever been in that establishment.

We found out later that it was the same at the Jewish club a few streets along the road. There must also have been a Salvation Army canteen somewhere as you could always rely on them, even where the fighting was, but we never had the need to find it in Durban.

Things had never been so good.

The next item on our agenda was a pint of the local beer. The trouble was that in Durban they had strange licensing hours, they were from 4pm until 6pm and it was after six so we had to settle for the cinema and back to the ship.

Before we docked at Durban they had given us £1 out of our pay books. My pay had mounted up a bit whilst on the ship for I was now on four shillings and sixpence a day (about 22p) as a leading aircraftsman and another few pence extra for passing the Observers' Course at St. Athan.

The food and the cinema were free so we hadn't had a bad day except for the chocolate.

The next day I went off the ship with Bob Kitching a lad from Lancaster and Ginger Speakman from Doncaster.

We spent most of our time lounging about on the sea front in the warmth of the afternoon and then off to try the Jewish club. It was the same carry on as the Catholic club except that we weren't asked to put our names in the book.

We had paced ourselves so that we would be in a bar before closing time. The bar we went into looked rough, reminiscent of saloons I had seen in American cowboy films. There were a few blokes in who looked as if they were on their way home from work. Most of them were standing about in small groups having a drink and a laugh before going home to their loved ones.

At a table in the corner of the room was a heavy built, rough looking chap with a cowboy hat on. There were also three empty chairs. As we looked a bit out of place standing there with our pints in our hands he asked us to come over and join him, which we did. I didn't like the look of him or the sound of him from the start. It wasn't long before he began telling us that we were going to Egypt and that we were going as cannon fodder and that the Germans were going to win at the end of the day.

He seemed to know a lot more than us for we had no idea where we were going and it had never crossed my mind that the Germans were going to win.

Then he came to the nitty gritty and the reason he had asked us to join him in the first place. He kept going on about cannon fodder and when he thought he'd got us worried he popped the question which was if any of us would jump the ship and go and work for him on his farm. We tried to explain to him that we knew nothing about farming. This made him laugh, when he got over his laughing he told us that we weren't expected to know anything about farming; all we would have to do was 'use the whip on the niggers.' I would have sooner used the whip on his big fat arse. None of us volunteered. I would take my chance with the German cannons and get home to Jean before being stuck in South Africa for the rest of my days.

It was day three and we were still tied up alongside the dock. At 12·30 we were off into town again with the rest of the day before us. Our first stop was the Jewish club where we had a nice pot of tea and a couple of buttered scones.

The next hour or so we spent sitting on the grass outside the city hall watching the rickshaws race past, and when I say race I mean literally racing. The Zulus who pulled them had them so well balanced that their bare feet hardly seemed to touch the ground, it was unbelievable.

I was with Bob and Ginger again. I don't know what had happened to Crowley. He had most likely been whisked off to some villa up in the hills to be wined and dined.

We were strolling along the sea front when a young black girl of about fifteen or sixteen walked passed us going our way, as she drew level with us she said in a quiet voice, 'Jig jig Johnny.' This method of conversation went on for about five hundred yards, first her slowing down, us going past and then the same thing again in reverse. Soon we had reached the end of the promenade with just beach and scrubland ahead. The exchange of words went something like this.

'Jig jig Johnny.'

'How much?'

'Half crown English.'

'Alright.'

'Follow me.'

It was me who had done the talking so it was me who followed her. Ginger and Bob seemed lost for words. She went on about fifty yards in front. She then disappeared into a little clearing at the top of the beach where it was out of sight to everyone.

There she was waiting for me and when I reached her she lay down on the sand, lifted her grubby white dress up, she hadn't any knickers on, and said, 'Come on Johnny you jig jig.' I looked down at her scrawny legs and then at her face that had no expression on it whatsoever.

There came over me a feeling of what I would now call shame. I thought of Jean and the little boy getting half a loaf of bread. I bent down pulled her dress down and said, 'No jig jig.'

She looked puzzled and stood up saying, 'You no like black girl?' I gave her five shillings. She stood there looking at me with tears running down her cheeks and said, 'You good boy, Johnny,' ran up the beach and disappeared into the bushes.

I found Bob and Ginger sat on a wall waiting for me. I joined them and we sat on the wall for a while in silence when all of a sudden Ginger said, 'You could go to prison for what you've just done.' Little did they know that Dave the lad was still a cock virgin and I didn't make them any the wiser.

Having walked quite a way along the sea front we decided to take a bus back into the town, go to the Catholic club for something to eat and then to a cinema.

At the bus stop were three Negroes waiting for the bus. When it stopped we told the Negroes to get on first as they were there first. The conductress on the bus got really angry with us and let us know in no uncertain manner that in South Africa the whites come first and not to forget it. I only hope that things have changed a lot since then for when all is said and done it was their country before the missionaries went there.

Next morning on the mess deck everyone knew that Dave had shagged a black girl. It's amazing how you can become famous without trying.

The next day was our last day in Durban and I must say that it had furthered my education extensively. We didn't know it was our last day as they have a theory in the services that the less the other ranks know the better.

Off we went again, up the hill from the docks and down into the town. By now we were beginning know our way around but for some reason we always finished up on Marine Drive. That afternoon, after lounging about for a bit, we strolled along, going nowhere, on the other side of the road from the promenade where all the posh hotels were. Most of them had balconies about shoulder high with a balustrade so as to give the people on the other side a bit of privacy.

We were wondering how to spend the rest of the day when a lady's voice from the balcony asked us if we would like to join her for afternoon tea. She told us to go to the main entrance and she would meet us there.

The hotel was called the Hotel Louie. I had never been in a place like this before and I don't think my two mates had either as all three of us were lost for words at the luxury of it all.

The lady introduced herself as Mrs McCormack. She had to ask us our names which made me feel a bit embarrassed but I was beginning to learn.

After our tea and scones with jam and cream we just sat there while Mrs M. made all the conversation, as I felt a bit out of my depth and I expect my pals felt the same. She told us her husband was an engineer and was working on a project just outside Durban. Their son was a captain in the army serving in Egypt.

After we had thanked her for the tea and scones she asked us if we would like to join her and her husband for dinner at seven o'clock.

It was a lovely meal but I didn't enjoy it as I was feeling self-conscious all the time and wondering if I was doing the proper things, like not making a noise whilst eating or not putting my elbows on the table or using the correct knives and forks etc.

On thanking her for dinner Mrs M. invited us to use the hotel for the rest of our stay in Durban and book any expenses to Mr M. who didn't have much to say. We couldn't take them up on their offer as we sailed next morning.

South Africa was just a blur on the horizon by the time I got on deck next morning.

I was back with Taffy and Ginger and we started giving the lifeboats a clean up and a coat of paint. Before we could start painting we had to fill the boat up to, or just above, the water line with sea water to swell the planks and tighten up the seams. It is amazing how much the timber had shrunk coming through the tropics. Besides passing the time on I was learning quite a bit about seamanship. Sometimes I wished I had joined the Merchant Navy. Though, on second thoughts, I don't know, as they lost more men than any other branch of the services.

d

6
India

On the second or third day from Durban we passed by Madagascar. The sea was like glass but there was a big swell and it was getting warmer as we were approaching the equator again. One morning, after about eight days at sea, we arrived in Bombay which since has been changed to Mumbai.

As we were going into dock I climbed up on to the table again and looked out of the porthole. The first thing I saw was a dead body floating past about twenty yards away. It always strikes me as strange the first things that come into your head on seeing things like this. My initial thought was 'why hasn't he sunk?'

I found out later that the sea is so buoyant in these places it is difficult to sink and, besides, the water was so filthy it looked as if you could walk on it.

Yes, we were now in the mysterious east and it brought back to my mind a few lines of one of the poems I had learned at school.

It was by Rudyard Kipling and went something like this:

Have you travelled east of Suez?
Where the best is like the worst
Where there ain't no ten commandments
And a man can raise a thirst.

We were leaving the 'Drunken Duchess' at Bombay. Rumour had it that we would be going across India to the Far East, as the Japanese had now come into the war. Like most rumours it was wrong which in service language was known as 'duff gen'.

I did get a pleasant surprise that morning when the bosun came to me and gave me a little brown envelope. It was my pay for the bit of work I'd done on the voyage. Seemingly the crew were all union men and there would have been trouble had I been working for nothing.

I couldn't believe my eyes when I opened the packet. There were eight crisp English pounds in it. I had not had that much money since saving up to go to Australia.

Our first day in India was a Sunday and as usual we were allowed ashore after tiffin. The famous gateway to India was there before us.

I had never heard of it before but I was thick. Frank seemed to be a bit of a knowledge box and explained to us what these big archways were – I wasn't greatly impressed.

What did impress me was the dazzling array of colours on the Marine Drive (yes, another Marine Drive). There were droves of ladies parading in their saris as it was Sunday afternoon.

We sauntered off into the town; had chicken and chips in a grotty café and I bought a birthday card to send to Jean when we got to wherever we were going to.

Next day I got a nice surprise as a sergeant came down on to the mess deck with a bag full of letters. It took him a long time to dish them out; when it came to mine I had ten from Jean and two from home.

I spent the rest of the day reading the letters over and over again, so I didn't get ashore that day. In one of the letters was a photograph of Jean which I have kept to this day.

After tea the deck sergeant came and told us to get our kits packed as we were leaving the ship next morning.

In the next dock there was an old peacetime troopship *The Nueralia*. It was a coal burner and looked as if it had been knocking about since the time of the Indian mutiny and on its decks we found ourselves later that morning.

There was a bit more room than we had on *The Duchess*, not that it mattered much for the weather was warm and I took to sleeping on the open deck.

The food was a lot better and at about four o'clock in the afternoon there was a nice pot of tea with white bread, butter and jam. We had never known such times.

If there were any crumbs on the mess table big cockroaches

would run out from behind the frames on the side of the ship, grab a crumb and run back with it.

We were now heading west towards the Persian Gulf and as usual there were rumours flying about all the time as to where we were going.

On about the third day out I had my first sight of an Arab dhow. I thought that I had never seen anything so lovely. There were three of them sailing along so gracefully it put me in mind of the swans which I had seen on the park lake as a boy.

I mentioned this to my pal Frank and he brought me down to earth when he said that they would most likely be carrying slaves from East Africa to sell in Arabia.

7
Iraq

After reaching the Persian Gulf I saw lots of sharks. The ones that fascinated me most were the Hammerheads. How evolution could fashion something so grotesque still beats me.

After about ten days we entered a wide river known as the Shatt al-Arab. It is fed by the Tigris and Euphrates rivers which meet about twenty miles or so up the Shatt al-Arab. It is said by some that at the fork where the two rivers meet was the site of the Garden of Eden.

On the right hand side of the river going up we saw Persia, now known as Iran. It was all desert except for the big oil refinery at Abadan. On our port side was Iraq which was lined with date palms all the way along the banks.

We disembarked at a place called Ashir, a suburb of Basra.

On disembarking we were laden down like donkeys, on our backs we had our backpack with a blanket round it wrapped up in a groundsheet. On our right-hand side was our small kit, which wasn't so small, next to that was our bayonet in a scabbard and on our left-hand side a water bottle which no one had said anything about filling before we left the ship.

With that lot and two kitbags, and the temperature at about forty degrees, it wasn't what you would call easy going.

On the dockside there was a little sergeant who must have been out there a week or two as his knees were brown.

'Right lads, follow me,' which was not easy as he wasn't loaded up and he went off at a brisk pace with us lot staggering along behind in a disorganised rabble trying to keep up with him.

After about half a mile the buildings petered out and we came to a clearing, beyond the clearing was just desert stretching away into the distance.

There was a large mud brick building with a door in it that may have been the ticket office at one time.

I was lucky and got a place sat on the sand with my back resting against the mud wall of the building.

The sun was hot on our heads even though we had our topees on. One of the lads suggested that we wore them back to front; the back protruded a bit more than the front so we did this and it worked as it kept the sun off our faces.

After what seemed a long time the little sergeant appeared back on the scene. In the meantime someone had suggested that by sucking small stones we would make saliva in our mouths and quench our thirst. The sergeant must have noticed this and it gave him the opportunity to give us a lecture on the folly of sucking stones. It went something like this.

'I have just noticed that some of you are sucking stones so as to pass the time on. I will give you a little talk about stone sucking.

'Let us say that in this area live about five hundred Arabs. We will estimate that each Arab has at least one shit per day. Multiply that by three hundred and sixty-five, then let us say that they have lived here for two thousand years, that gives us a sum of 500 x 365 x 2000. That means that every stone around these parts has been used at least once in its lifetime to scrape the clinkers from around an Arab's arsehole and you dirty buggers are sucking at them as if they were Aunt Sally's humbugs.'

At last it came. A decrepit looking old engine pushing a few metal cattle trucks down the line towards us. With a lot of banging, clanking, smoke and steam shooting out all over the place, it came to a halt.

The sergeant had disappeared again. When he returned he had two Arabs who were pulling a cart. On the cart were about half a dozen dixies. They began by emptying packets of tea, sugar and tins of condensed milk into the dixies. I was wondering where they would get boiling water from but I didn't have to wonder for long as there was a tap or valve on the front of the engine.

As one Arab filled the dixies with boiling water the other one was stirring the contents up with a big stick.

'Right lads, form a queue and bring your mess tins.'

It was our first meal since getting off the ship and it was now about five o'clock.

A mess tin of tea that looked a bit oily with bits of rust floating about on top, a tin of melted down bully beef (corned beef) and a packet of hard tack (ships' biscuits).

I didn't see anybody leave any.

The sergeant told us we were going to Baghdad and the train could only travel during the night as the rails got distorted by the heat and we could sleep on the sleepers during the day when the train was stationary.

No one laughed at his little joke.

After piling into the trucks with our kit, a box of corned beef, Maconochie meat and vegetable stew, tea, sugar and milk we found ourselves rocking and rolling our way to Baghdad. The next day we stopped near the Hanging Gardens of Babylon. I didn't bother to look at them. Some of the lads that did said I hadn't missed much.

All day long there were dozens of children crying out to us for corned beef and stew. The masses of flies around their eyes didn't seem to trouble them. Little did we know that it wouldn't be long before we would be in the same state.

I am not sure but I think that we had one more stop before we reached Baghdad. I seem to recollect names of places like Ur of the Caldeas and Abraham's Mount.

On arriving at Baghdad there was a convoy of wagons awaiting us not far from the station. The drivers were sat on the ground at the side of the wagons waiting for us to sort ourselves out and get on board. I got talking to the driver of our wagon, he was a bit of a killjoy and seemed to know much more about how the war was going on than a lot of the generals.

According to him our troops had retreated again in Egypt and the German army was ready to cross the Nile, which meant they would go through the Middle East like a dose of salts. He said the Russians wouldn't hold out much longer at Stalingrad and when it fell the German army would sweep down through Iran and meet up with their pals in Iraq.

He didn't tell me what was going to happen to us whilst all this was going on. What he did tell me was we were going to a transit camp about forty miles away called Habbaniyah. The camp was on the side of the main road, which in those days was just a track in the sand.

The main camp and airfield of Habbaniyah was about half a mile away with a tall metal fence round its perimeter. It was said the luxury of the place was out of this world.

The airmen on the camp had their own swimming pool, a cinema, even a servant boy to clean their billet and wash their clothes, and a riding school. God alone knows what the officers had.

After having a brew, the usual tin of bully and a packet of biscuits we were allotted our tents and told to have a good rest as we had to be on parade next morning at 6am. We were to work erecting tents until nine o'clock and continue again in the evening from five until seven. It was too hot for us to be expected to work during the day.

We were thrown in at the deep end with the tent building. We were given the job of building one for a NAAFI. It was made from about a dozen tents joined together making a kind of marquee.

If you have read the book *Adolf Hitler: My Part in His Downfall* by Spike Milligan you will know all about the finer points and pitfalls encountered in tent building as he described it much better than I can.

I had no idea until now how many more living creatures there are on this earth than us humans. Millions of over-friendly flies, black scorpions, yellow scorpions, big scorpion spiders, chameleons that changed colour to match their background, lizards, hyenas that laughed the whole night long, packs of pyeards (wild dogs) which could smell an open tin of corned beef from a mile away and many more of God's creatures that he created to make life unpleasant for us mere humans.

There was a standpipe with a tap where we could get water but the pipe to the tap ran on the top of the ground so by the time it reached the tap it was boiling hot.

Outside each of our tents we had what they called a chatty. It was a large porous ceramic jar supported in a wooden frame. The idea was that the hot wind blowing through the pores in the jar kept the water cool just the same as the pores in our skin are our cooling system when we sweat and the wind blows against our body. The trouble is that with fair skinned people their pores are not as open as dark skinned ones and they stop sweating which ends up with them suffering from heat exhaustion.

On the second morning after we had finished work on the tents, Mr Newell our commanding officer, called us out on parade. He began by telling us how the unit would function when operating.

There would be sixteen posts with six men to each post, making a total of ninety-six, and as there were one hundred and fifty men on the unit the other fifty-four would be headquarters; i.e. storemen, mechanics, drivers, wireless ops, cooks and reserves for the posts.

A post would consist of three observers, two wireless opps. and a driver; the driver doing the cooking, one of the observers would be a corporal in charge off the post.

The observers who had experience as gunners and were leading aircraftsmen would be promoted to corporal. This worked out just right as there were eighteen such men, that meant one for each post and two in reserve, so I was promoted to corporal and it was left to me to sort my other five men out.

I finished up with Harry Birkenhead as driver, Yoddy Mills and Harry Clark wireless opps., Archie Osborne and Ralph Needham as observers.

Harry, the driver, came from Manchester; he was forty-two years old and lost no time in telling me that he had a daughter older than me.

Yoddy, a taffy, joined up as a boy when he was sixteen so he was a good wireless opp.

Harry Clark came from Warrington and had been a butcher in civvy street (which came in useful later).

Archie was the drollest of the bunch. He had come straight from Glasgow University into the air force, he spoke French and German fluently, had refused a commission, drank all the booze he could lay his hands on and was a devout communist.

All I can say about Ralph was that he came from Todmorden and was a good singer. He wasn't with us long.

Things were happening all at the same time.

The drivers had to go and collect wagons from the main camp. The wagons were Ford three tonners with a V8 engine and four wheel drive. There was a round hole in the top of the cab with a metal rod around it to mount a Lewis machine gun on. With the engine box being inside the cab the idea was for the man operating the gun to stand on the engine box with his head and shoulders through the hole and fire away.

The next job was to go to the main camp and draw the equipment for what was to be our home for the next year or so. A few WOUs must have passed through Habbaniyah before us for when we got to the store on the main camp it seemed to be highly organised.

A long row of trestle tables with a store basher behind each one, behind the store men were shelves full of everything bar the kitchen sink. When we went into the store they lent us a cart to carry the equipment back to the wagon.

What puzzled me was how we were going to pack all this stuff on to the wagon and us besides. There were things like cooking gear, mule tanks for water, a Bell steriliser, two tents, ammunition and a tin bath that we never used. Besides all this there was the wireless equipment – a transmitter and receiver along with a generator, batteries, charging motor and a thirty-foot aerial mast. It was all bunged into the wagon to be sorted out later.

After breakfast the next morning Shorty Frost, the CO's batman, came round the tents to tell us that Andy (Mr Newell's Christian name) wanted us all on parade for rifle inspection in ten minutes. This came as a bit of a shock as I don't think any of us had thought of cleaning our rifles since we got on the ship at Liverpool.

There we were all lined up looking a bit guilty, along came Andy and gave the order 'Port arms for inspection'.

At the order you bring the rifle up from the order arms position to a diagonal position across your chest and pull the bolt back, when the officer gets to you and stands facing you, you bring the rifle forward and place the thumb of your right hand over the head of the bolt so that the light coming down the barrel reflects off your thumb nail, he cocks his eye and looks down the barrel.

I could hear him further down the line accusing some of the lads of having spider's webs down their barrels, intermingled with lots of four letter words.

It looked as if we were going to be busy with our oil and four by two cleaning the barrels with our pull-throughs. I was wrong. When he had finished telling us what a slovenly lot we were he told us to fire a round or two to clear the shit out of our barrels.

Five minutes later it sounded as if the battle of Waterloo had started all over again.

Sirens were whining out on the main camp and they had closed the big metal gates. We heard later that they thought that Rashid Ali and his private army had attacked the camp again.

Frank Smith 'Smithie', one of the lads in our tent, had started passing out at about ten o'clock each morning with heat exhaustion so we had to take it in turns throughout the day until about four o'clock putting wet towels on him to make up for him not sweating. There was no air conditioning in those days.

We had by this time got into a kind of routine.

At half past four, when the temperature had dropped to below a hundred, a few of us would stagger over the hill to 'Lake Habbaniyah' where Harry Clark was teaching me to swim. I'd never learned to swim at school as we had a choice between swimming and woodwork and I chose woodwork.

In the evening, before we went to the canteen, I would wrestle with a big lad called Ginger Watson just to entertain the lads. He had done some all-in wrestling before he joined up so he taught me a few tricks of the trade. The main one was to make it look good without hurting each other. Some of lads must have thought we were serious as one morning Andy sent for us both, made us shake hands and told us that he wasn't going to have any fighting on this unit unless we met up with any Germans or Yanks. He must have thought it strange as Ginger was about twice my size.

About a week had gone by and we had started wondering when we were going to move on as it was only a transit camp, and as always happens in the forces there were plenty of rumours flying about. Some were that we were going up north to Kurdistan. Others were that we were going across to Egypt to join the North African campaign, and as usual they were wrong.

One morning Geordie Lawson, a wireless opp., asked me if I fancied hitch-hiking into Baghdad with him. It was scorching hot but off we went.

Getting there was no problem as there were plenty of army wagons going that way.

Going over the bridge in Baghdad we saw boys diving off the bridge for coins, how they found them was a miracle as the water was the colour of mud but they never failed to come up with the coin.

All the people seemed to be going one way so we followed the crowd.

Eventually we came to a large open space where the crowd was gathering. All around the space were stalls selling food, rugs and all sorts of things that you find on market days.

In the middle of the clearing was a stout post about three feet high sticking up out of the ground. A group of soldiers standing by us must have thought that we looked a bit puzzled. 'Do you know what's going on mate?' one asked. We didn't. He then told us that there was to be a public execution at twelve o'clock. It was about half past eleven and as we had a good place near the front we decided to stay and watch, which was going to be difficult with the sweat running down off our eyebrows and into our eyes.

Just before twelve two big brawny Arabs dragged a little thin scrawny chap out to the post in the middle of the square with what looked like the town dignitaries following on behind.

Everyone was cheering; that was everyone except the unfortunate little fellow with the main part of course. He was hobbled and his hands were tied behind his back.

When the two big fellas got him to the post they sat him cross legged with his back against the post and tied him to it with his head and neck just clearing the top of the post. All of a sudden there was an enormous cheer as into the arena walked the executioner.

He carried an axe over his shoulder as if it was a rifle. It was a long pole with a large curved blade on the end.

Without any messing about he took up his position and with one mighty sideways swing the little chap's head was off, it fell on to the ground in front of him.

Besides me nearly being sick, what I remember most about the whole thing was the distance that the blood shot up into the air when his head came off.

A voice behind me said, 'Let's go.' It was Geordie, who must have felt the same way as I did. All he said as we walked away was 'Never again.'

We strolled along not knowing where we were going but trying to keep our sense of direction so we didn't get lost. Every time we were passing a coffee shop we went in and had a glass of limoon to try and replace the sweat we were losing.

We were standing at a corner not knowing which way to go

when a big African lady standing in a doorway a few yards away down the street beckoned to us saying, 'Jig jig Johnny?' How did they all know my name?

When we showed a bit of interest she explained to us as best she could that she had got a new girl so she was very cheap at 250 fils (25p).

I said that it was too hot but Geordie was all for it and in he went.

After he had gone in the madam asked me if I would like to see an exhibition upstairs for 50 fils so up I went.

The floors in these buildings were constructed of floorboards on beams with no plaster ceiling underneath.

In the room were about half a dozen soldiers lying face down on the floor squinting with one eye through holes in the floorboards. One of the soldiers turned round when he heard me come into the room, putting a finger to his lips telling me not to make a noise.

I found myself a hole and got down with the rest of them.

What a sight! There was the girl sat on the bed and there was Geordie with just his socks on. As he went to get hold of her, she spun round and rolled across the bed to get out of his reach. He ran round to the other side of the bed and she rolled back the other way. These antics went on for about five minutes and the sweat was by now pouring off him.

Across from the foot of the bed was a large solid looking chest of drawers. By this time the girl was stood up on the foot of the bed opposite the chest of drawers. Geordie went to grab her legs but she jumped over him on to the top of the drawers. He made a grab for her legs again but she jumped over him on to the bed and lay there exhausted with her legs wide open. Geordie immediately fell on top of her and hid his sausage.

I waited for him outside. When he came out he looked as if he had just done fifteen rounds with Joe Lewis.

As we walked down the street he was too knackered to speak for a while. When he did he explained to me what a carry on he had with her being new to the game. I let him go on a while. When I could get a word in I mentioned that it was a good bit when she jumped off the bed and on to the chest of drawers.

He stopped in his tracks and looked at me with a bewildered look on his face.

'How do you know?'

'I was watching you from upstairs along with a company of squaddies.'

He was quiet for a while. When he did speak it was in a kind of a sheepish voice, 'You won't tell the lads when we get back to camp will you?'

I didn't.

Another day or two at Habbaniyah and we were on our way again.

With us now having our own transport we were an independent unit and more or less self supporting. We even had our own water tanker called a bowser. It was a three hundred gallon tank mounted on a trailer and towed by a Crossley wagon.

No one informed us as to where we were going but we knew that we were heading for Baghdad.

About fifty miles south of Baghdad was our first stop for the night.

Johnny Danvers, the unit cook, and his mate Taffy Hughes, who was in charge of the rations, dumped about two hundred tins of Maconochie's meat and vegetable stew into a dozen dixies, dug a shallow trench, made a fire in the trench with camel thorn and in no time at all we were having what was for a long time to be our evening meal along with a packet of biscuits and a pot of tea.

Not having had the time to sort ourselves out for sleeping in the wagon we were rolling our bed rolls out by the side of the wagon and sleeping there with our kitbags for pillows.

After another two days travelling on roads that were more or less tracks in the sand we arrived at another transit camp called Shiba.

At Shiba there were the remains of what looked like a harbour although it was about ten miles from the nearest water. It was said to be the harbour that Sinbad the sailor sailed from.

It was hotter than anywhere we had ever been, the sand was blowing all the time making the sun look like a copper ball in the sky.

An old sailor who had travelled the world once told me that if you had been to Shiba then you would go to heaven as you had already been to hell.

After a day or two Bill Conner got me on my own and asked

me if I would go into Basra with him and show him how to go on regarding the brothels.

It seemed that after my capers in Durban I was now an authority on such matters. I didn't know whether to be ashamed or flattered so I volunteered.

So off into Basra we went and the only thing I could do was play it by ear.

We stood on the corner of two grubby looking streets and in no time at all a garry (horse drawn taxi) pulled up and the driver asked us if we wanted 'jig jig'.

I haggled about the price for a while until he finally agreed to take us. The journey seemed to take us down the same streets a few times. Maybe it was to make it look a long way for our money or more likely it was to make sure that we wouldn't find the brothel again under our own steam.

There was a door let into an old mud brick wall where the driver banged three times and went on his way. He would collect his commission later.

A big fat Arab woman came to the door, had a quick look up and down the street, pulled us through the doorway and up the stairs.

Before we even set eyes on the girls she wanted five hundred fils (50p) off each of us.

I was feeling a bit nervous and I could tell by the look on Bill's face that he was on the verge of changing his mind.

Up another flight of steps we went and there in the doorway of a room was a plump Arab girl who looked to be well on the top side of twenty-five summers. Before anyone could protest she grabbed hold of Bill, pulled him in and closed the door.

Off I went with the madam up another flight of steps and on to a flat roof with just a bed and a chair on it. The girl looked about sixteen and a bit underfed. She told me to sit on the chair, knelt down in front of me and in a much practised way removed my shorts.

After entertaining me with the starters she got on the bed with her frock up to her neck and her legs wide open calling, 'Come on Johnny, jig jig.'

There were no flashing lights or thinking that I was in heaven and it was all over in two minutes.

When I got outside there was Bill waiting for me, his face as red as a beetroot, not from the heat or embarrassment but with anger.

He kept saying, ‘What about Peg?’ and ‘What if I’ve got a dose?’ He seemed to be blaming me for it all. I was having the same thoughts about Jean.

I lost a good pal in Bill, as our friendship was never the same after that day, so I made a resolution that I would never assist anyone in their carnal desires again.

8
Kuwait

Two days later we were on the move again and still heading south. Shorty Frost the CO's batman said that he had heard a place called El-Kuwait mentioned, none of us had ever heard of it.

After bumping along on another sandy track (that will probably now be a six lane motorway) for a few hours it was brewing up time. It was so hot that the water was nearly boiling when it came out of the container.

It was late afternoon when at last we saw the city of El-Kuwait shimmering in the heat haze.

The walls of the city were about half a mile away, the beach and the sea about one hundred yards to our left where there were some Arabs working on a dhow. The beach was the local boat building yard.

Andy, our CO, told us to form the wagons up in a circle with the back ends facing inwards and to work a night guard roster out amongst ourselves. It wasn't the Arabs he was worried about, it was the packs of hyenas and wild dogs which were prowling about all over the place, maybe they could smell the Maconochie's stew that we were eating out of the tins. And like the tea it didn't need heating.

We were all dog tired so it was bed rolls by the side of the wagons and an early night for we knew that we would be up at dawn in the morning and making camp before the temperature started to soar.

As usual in the forces the cookhouse tent was the first, then the stores and last of all our twelve foot by twelve foot tents which were to be our living quarters when not operating as posts.

In two or three days we had the camp finished and functional and Andy had arranged with the boat builders on the beach to supply us with timber to build bunks in our wagons. Later on in our travels they were a godsend.

On arriving at Kuwait the CO had us on parade and informed us that our job there was to patrol the northern part of the Persian Gulf aboard dhows that had been borrowed from the pearling fleet.

The main intention of the operation was to keep a lookout for Japanese submarines the powers that be thought could be making their way into the Gulf. We also had to plot aircraft and shipping and give weather reports; not that the weather ever changed much.

The city of Kuwait itself looked like a set from a French Foreign Legion film. It was then a walled city with the wall made from mud bricks, as were all the other buildings in the city.

There were only two motor vehicles in the place. They were two Humber shooting brakes. One belonged to the Sheik and the other one belonged to the political agent, as Kuwait was a British mandated territory in those days. If my memory serves me right I seem to remember that he was a man from Huddersfield called Shaw.

The entrance to the city was through a pair of great big double doors that were opened at 6am and closed at 6pm.

The Sheikh did not allow the people to have a cinema or books and magazines from the outside world as he thought that it would make the people dissatisfied if they saw how other people lived, or maybe he didn't want them corrupted by the western way of life. There was no alcohol in any shape or form.

The Bedouin nomads slept in their black tents outside the wall as it was against their custom to sleep in a house or town. The currency in those days was Indian and the water was one anna per gallon. It was brought to Kuwait in tanks on dhows from Basra in Iraq and pumped manually into a big storage tank. This was at the top of the beach where we were camped so our water supply was no problem.

In the mornings before the heat became too intense the Kuwaiti women, who were heavily veiled, would come to the tank with their goatskin bags for their daily ration of water.

Some of the lads from HQ would boast to those of us on the dhows when we went ashore that for a gallon of water some of the women had been known to let them have a look at their faces.

The main industries in Kuwait in those days were pearling and slave trading. The pearling was just slaving in another form for after a couple of seasons that only lasted a few months the divers, who started diving as young boys, ended up in pawn to the dhow owners, for in the close season they had to borrow money from them in order to keep alive. They then had to pay the money back out of next season's wages, which wasn't a lot.

Not many of them lived to the age of thirty for if the sharks didn't get them or their lungs didn't burst there was always the bends.

They did what is known as free diving whereby they went down holding their nose with one hand and in the other hand they had a basket with a couple of stones in it to help them stay down on the sea bed. They would then fill the basket with oysters, give a tug on the line and one of the crew hoisted it up on to the deck. The diver then shot up to the surface with such force that sometimes his whole body seemed to come out of the water, hence the danger of the dreaded bends.

The dhows used for the slaving travelled quite a long way for their cargo. They went down the Gulf, then down the east coast of Africa as far as Mombasa and Zanzibar.

The slave market was held on a Tuesday afternoon so if a boat-load of slaves came into the harbour on a Wednesday and had to wait six days the stench coming up out of the hold became a bit unpleasant.

It was a pitiful sight to see. Men, women and children brought up on to the harbour side on Tuesday morning and washed down to make them look presentable for the bidding in the afternoon. Many of the boys would be made into eunuchs in what was a nasty operation during which many of them died.

All this was going on in what was then a British Mandate about seventy years ago before the oil got flowing.

On the dhow we had an interpreter called Solomon, 'Solli' for short, whose job was to translate my orders, received by wireless, to the captain saying where to go etc. The captain was in charge of the sailing with a crew of six.

At the beginning of the first voyage we did our own cooking. One day Abdullah the cook invited us to have the evening meal with them. It soon came about that we pooled our rations and all sat on the deck around a big tray eating with our fingers. It didn't take long before we came to the conclusion that knives and forks were surplus to requirements.

Not once did any of the crew ask if the corned beef or Maconochie's stew was halal (slaughtered in the Muslim method).

In the evening Solli would sit with us on the deck and teach us a bit of Arabic, which I found came in very handy at times later on our travels.

The evenings were lovely when the heat of the day was gone and the temperature dropped to about 90°F.

With the sails filling in the soft warm breeze and the dhow gliding along as if it was in space I realised then that I had fallen in love with boats and the sea. What I didn't realise at the time was that we don't often get conditions like that around our green and pleasant land.

Solli was unhappy with the carry-on in Kuwait. The trouble was that he had been educated at Basra where he had learned to speak English. The majority of the other people in Kuwait seemed to be content enough. It makes me wonder sometimes if education is all that it is cracked up to be.

The first place we called in on our first voyage was Bahrain. It was then an island just off the coast but since they have built a causeway across along with all the big flash hotels etc.

The Emir told us that we shouldn't swim in the sea because of the sharks so he set some of his labourers to work digging or chopping a little swimming pool out of the coral. He said that it would be finished next time we came but it wasn't.

We only did one more trip and never a Japanese submarine in sight.

A day or two before we got back to Kuwait a motor launch belonging to the Sheik came out to us with some mail and rations. There were a few letters from Jean and two from home. One of the letters from Jean said she had joined the WAAFs thinking that by doing so she may meet up with me sometime.

The corporal who looked after delivering and collecting the mail was an ex-public school boy with a double-barrelled name;

why he hadn't been given a commission I never found out.

He took our mail for home and the money for the stamps. It came to light later that he had been throwing the letters in the sea and pocketing the money for the stamps.

With the kind of life we had it wasn't feasible to dole out the usual type of punishment so Andy the CO took him two or three hundred yards from the camp behind some sand hills and gave him a good hiding. He bore the scars for a long time after.

You may have noticed earlier in the story that I had done some dodgy things but I think what that corporal did could be called scraping the bottom of the barrel.

It was only a few days after coming back from our second voyage that we broke camp and were on our way again.

During those few days we built six bunks in the wagon with the planks that Andy had bought from the boat builders.

I never knew anything about Andy's background or education but what I did know was that he wasn't lacking in common sense.

Before we left Kuwait the dhow was tied up alongside the harbour wall and someone had managed to get hold of some white paint and a brush, gone down to the harbour and painted 'The Good Ship Syphilis' on the bow of the boat. It wasn't long before I was known as 'Captain Gonorrhoea' of the Good Ship Syphilis. It was soon shortened to 'Captain Gun' and it stuck with me for a long time, which brings to my mind a funny story, so I will digress for a few lines.

A few years later and I was a private soldier in the Green Howards. The Second World War had finished and I was in Cyprus where more trouble had flared up. A lot of water had gone under the bridge since my days at Kuwait. A lot of it was murky water but that's yet another story.

I was stationed at Dekelia near Larnaca. One night I was having a drink in the canteen with some of the lads when who should walk in but Smithie who had been one of the observers on my post in North Africa. He must have been misbehaving himself somewhere along the line to have finished up in the army like myself but we didn't go into details.

At first I thought how good it was to see one of my old pals again, until I remembered a nasty incident in Tunisia which he and the other four members of the post knew about but I thought had been dead and buried along with thousands of other nasty incidents that happen in war.

His first words were, 'Well if it ain't my old mate Captain Gun.'

The lads with me looked a bit puzzled as they knew me by my old nickname 'Dave' and as it happened the name of our company officer was Captain Gunn. It didn't take long before he sent for me and wanted to know what it was all about, so I told him the story.

At first I don't think he believed me, then after I had filled him in with a few more details he seemed convinced. And he must have been impressed for the next day he sent for me and said that with my experience I was wasting my time as a private and 'From now on you will be addressed as Cpl. Davidson and not as Captain Gun as there is only room for one Captain Gunn in this battalion.'

I could have told him that, according to the book, a man cannot be promoted within six months of him being reduced to the ranks. I didn't tell him, as officers don't like their inferiors quoting the book to them.

To carry on with my story I will return to Kuwait where we stayed for another few days, then off we went again back to Shaiba and Basra. The rumours were flying around again that we were going to Egypt, which wasn't so good as things weren't going too well there at the time. The rumours as usual were wrong again for when we arrived at Basra we headed east across the Shatt al-Arab.

The method used to get us across the river was by means of a big raft with a tugboat lashed alongside.

It took a long time to get the wagons, equipment and us across and about three trips.

I was on the last trip and it was getting dark; all had gone well until that final crossing. Bang in the middle of the river the tug parted company with the raft which went floating off down the river out of control. The officer in charge of the raft seemed to be at a loss as to what to do. The Arab raft sailors were all running up and down shouting at each other. We lads couldn't do anything for laughing.

Finally it all got sorted out and we set our feet on the not so fair land of Persia (Iran).

9

Iran and Russia

The first hundred and fifty miles or so when entering Iran by crossing the Shatt al-Arab is the Persian desert, which is not difficult to describe as it is just like any other desert.

On the first night we got bedded down by the side of the wagons. It was the first time that I had felt cold for a long time. In the morning we were up early, collecting camel thorn to light fires which we sat round eating porridge with our blankets around us.

By nine o'clock we were bumping along with the sweat pouring off us. Such contrasts in temperature were unbelievable. The atmosphere was so clear that when only half way across the desert I could see the first range of mountains in the distance.

The next night we camped outside an oil town called Awhas. The oil wells were manned mostly by Yanks who didn't seem too friendly, or maybe it was because British servicemen had no time for Americans in those days. It most likely had something to do with them shagging their wives and girlfriends back in Blighty.

The terrain of Iran seemed to consist of a range of mountains, then between each range was a flat agricultural plain of about ten to twenty miles. This carried on to the last range north of Tehran, the Elburz Mountains that finish at the Caspian sea and Russia.

The frightening bit was that we were heading that way.

Each night our CO, Andy, made sure we made camp on a plain because of the intense cold on the mountains.

All went well until one afternoon when the convoy was

nearing the top of a range before a town called Qum when the big end bearing went on the wagon towing the trailer with the water tank on it.

It was decided that we stay there for the night whilst the mechanics stripped the engine down and replaced the bearing. It must have been a gruelling task in the icy conditions.

None of us others slept that night; we collected any fuel that we could find and sat huddled around the fires in our blankets.

At Qum there was an impressive looking Muslim shrine known as ‘Queen Fatima’s Tomb’.

The next day we reached the city of Tehran.

Compared with other Eastern cities Tehran was a pleasant looking place. The streets were laid out in a grid pattern making it easy for you to find your way about. What fascinated me most were the streams that ran down the sides of the tree-lined streets.

The streams came down from the Elburz mountains and across the plain to the north of the city, some of them through man-made tunnels that looked as if they had been built thousands of years ago.

We made our camp a mile or so to the north of the city on the road to the town of Karach. Our camp was on the north side of the road, a little way to the south was an airfield called Mehrabad.

Running alongside the camp was an open stream so we were all right for water.

The first job after pitching the tents was to dig a latrine that was about eight feet long by three feet wide with a strong pole resting on a tripod at each end of the trench.

Our next job was to build six bunks in the wagon. The wagon was going to be our abode for a long time to come. The layout of the wagon was something like this:

In the cab were the driver’s seat and passenger seat, between the seats was the engine cover and, as mentioned before, in the roof of the cab was a circle cut out with a lid that folded back; round the circle was a steel rod on which to mount the Lewis machine gun. Whoever was manning the gun stood on the engine box with his head and shoulders through the hole and hoped that he was only shooting at ducks. In between the cab and the covered in part of the wagon was a space with the spare wheel in it; over the spare wheel we draped our two tents. On the outside on one side was a mule tank and on the other side were the metal tracks for getting us through soft sand. The mule tank was for storing water and it was called a mule tank because in wars gone by transportation of water was done by mules carrying a tank slung on either side of the animal. At the top end, inside the covered in part, was the wireless transmitter/receiver complete with batteries, charging motor etc. Together with all this stuff was the cooking equipment with a stove which we never used much as we preferred to cook on fires (not that we had much to cook anyway) and all the other things it takes for six men to live in luxury.

After two or three days there was a nasty accident. Johnny Danvers, the cook, had two jobs, cooking and looking after the latrine (what you could call taking care of both ends), had, with the heat of the sun combined with the heat of the cookhouse, gone a bit doolally (mentally unstable) and a trifle absentminded.

After breakfast when he had sorted things out in the cookhouse he saw to the latrine, a task that entailed him in taking a can of petrol, pouring it into the trench and then throwing a lighted match in. Then he finished it off with a layer of lime to make it smell nice and sweet.

On this particular morning after he had poured the petrol in he found that he had forgotten the matches, so off he trotted back to the cookhouse to get them. When he returned a large amount of petrol vapour had built up in the trench.

In went the match and up went the contents of the latrine and down into the hole went Henry Cook, a lad that happened to be sitting on the pole when Danny threw the match in.

The first thing was the explosion and then Henry's screams. Our tent was nearest the latrine which was all right if you were taken short in the night so we were first on the scene.

There were still a lot of flames about but even in our panic we somehow managed to get him out of the hole. Someone dashed off to get a tube of tannic acid jelly from the first aid box to put on his burns, which were bad.

Whilst we were doing this our CO and Shorty his bat-man turned up in a fifteen hundredweight van and whisked him off to the military hospital in Tehran.

We didn't see Henry again.

The next morning Andy had us on parade and said that the dogs that some of the lads had picked up on our journey would

e

have to be destroyed as the posts would be heading off towards Russia in the next day or two. He also inspected our rifles again and we all got a bollocking. Before he dismissed us he told me to report to him in his tent.

I felt out of place as the only other times I had confronted an officer on my own was when I had been on charges and even then there was always an escort with you.

In his tent were two folding chairs and a table; on the table was a pile of letters waiting to be censored and a file with my name and number on it. He told me to sit down and by the look on his face I could tell that he was going to read the riot act to me.

'Right Cpl. Davidson, I have here in front of me your records which have just caught up with you and if I had seen them before you wouldn't be wearing those two stripes; on the other hand whilst you have been on this unit you seem to have kept your nose clean.'

I thought that I had got away scot-free but no, in the next breath he said, 'You and that Communist pal of yours, Osborne, can shoot the dogs tomorrow morning.'

As I was leaving the tent he called me back and told me that if I hadn't jumped the ship at Liverpool I would now have been in Ceylon because that was where my records had come from. It looked as if they had gone on the ship without me.

The next morning Archie and I took the dogs away from the camp and shot them. The look in their eyes when I pulled the trigger haunted me for a long time and it made me hope that I would never have to shoot humans.

There was a certain amount of coolness between some of the lads with Archie and me for a long time after; in fact I think that some of them thought that we had volunteered for the job and that we had enjoyed it. To make things worse one of the dogs belonged to my old brothel pal Bill Connor.

What a week that was.

Before leaving Tehran we got the order never to use tannic acid jelly for burns again, nobody told us what we did have to use.

Two days after the dog shooting I was given ordnance maps covering the Elburz Mountains and the southern coast of the Caspian Sea.

As the Germans still had Stalingrad under siege and were ready to take Grozny at any minute, things didn't look too good for Captain Gun and his merry men.

Going over the Elburz Mountains was quite an experience. The road was just a gravel track hewn out of the mountain side which followed a river up to the summit. At times the river was just a silver thread hundreds of feet below; what made it more frightening was that every now and again we would meet with Russian wagons coming the other way and with us being on the 'downhill' side of the road it didn't make things any easier. The Russian soldiers were a friendly easy-going lot so we always found a way of making room to pass.

The Russian wagons were in convoys of about five or six and were carrying arms and equipment from the Persian Gulf all the way up to the Russian front; on the headboards of the wagons was a Union Jack at one end and the hammer and sickle at the other end with the letters UKCC.

One of the soldiers who spoke a little English told us that it was a joint effort between Russia and Britain for getting American arms to the Russian front.

Later on we were surprised how many of them could speak English, especially the officers, maybe they taught English at the universities.

On our first night in the mountains we pulled in on a flat bit at the side of the road, lit a fire, heated up six tins of stew, topped up our mule tank from the river and sat round the fire drinking tea and telling tales before retiring to our bunks that we had built at Tehran.

I didn't bother putting on a guard as everything seemed so nice and peaceful.

I had just got off to sleep when Harry Birkenhead woke me up and whispered that he had heard feet padding around the wagon. I looked out and it all seemed nice and quiet but he insisted that it was a bear and that we should keep the flaps tied down.

I told him that he was imagining things and as he always did when he got riled with me he informed me that he had a daughter older than me.

Harry was a grand old chap; what he was doing out here at the age of forty-two was a mystery to me. All I could think of was that he must have volunteered; people are apt to do silly things in times of war so I never asked him.

The next day we carried on towards the summit, which I

estimated to be about seven or eight thousand feet, and it was beginning to feel much colder. At about two thousand feet from the summit, which was still covered in snow from the previous winter, there was a tunnel that took the road through the mountain.

At this end of the tunnel was an Iranian checkpoint and at the other end was a Russian checkpoint; this puzzled me because according to our maps the Russian border was much further north.

It was now all downhill. After going down for an hour or so we were lost in cloud. Before we entered the cloud the terrain was just rugged mountains with a solitary pine tree here and there. The difference when we came down out of the cloud was amazing. Now it was forest with lovely green trees and grass which I hadn't seen since we left England. There were small groups of people working in the forest chopping trees down. As we went past they just stood and stared at us. I found out later that both men and women from one little village would work as a team. The system was that they would chop down a tree, lop off the branches and cut it up into logs. The smaller branches were stacked into kilns and made into charcoal. The logs were taken down to the coast and used as fuel for the boilers on the small ships. The Russians didn't waste much either in labour or materials.

The trunks of the trees were sawn up into planks and it looked like hard work to me. The method they used looked a bit primitive and it worked like this. There was a trench about six feet deep with a tripod at each end where the tree trunk rested; down each side of trunk was a plank which the operator at the top stood on with a foot at each side of the trunk. The saw was double-ended so that one person was on the top and one in the trench getting the sawdust in their eyes; it looked as if it worked on a man and wife basis with the wife always in the trench.

I talked it over with the lads and we decided to carry on down to the coast instead of spending the night in the forest.

Harry the driver didn't seem to mind, so we went to our first designated position near a little town called Chaloos on the coast of the Caspian Sea.

When it got dark there were hundreds of little lights in the bushes at the side of the road. We found out later that they were glow-worms.

On arriving at Chaloos we set our stall for the first time since leaving Kuwait.

That evening Harry Clark and Yoddy did the first collective call on the wireless; we did the collective calls at six o'clock in the morning and six in the evening. Anything else we saw at other times i.e. aircraft, shipping when near the sea, weather reports was all done in morse code as we weren't allowed to use plain language. It was also all to be decoded from our code book and the code was changed every three weeks. The signal wasn't very strong and Harry said it was because of the mountains between us and Tehran. This was strange because he discovered that by putting F coils in the receiver we could get the BBC on the head phones. There would have been trouble if we had been found out but with me tending to be on the religious side I was still a firm believer in the eleventh commandment which is 'thou shalt not get caught'. Admittedly, looking back on my past experiences, I have sinned a few times by breaking it.

It was great being able to listen to Vera Lynn, the Robinson family and the news. We found we could amplify the sound by putting each of the headphones into our enamel mugs.

We had two or three days at Chaloos that were very pleasant. We were able to have a haircut at the barbers and a shower at the silk factory which even in those times had showers and a canteen for the workers. We didn't have to pay for anything. I found out later that the Russian soldiers didn't pay for anything. They wouldn't be able to as their pay was only a few kopeks a day which worked out at about tuppence.

We had just got settled in when three Russian soldiers came to see us. They were as drunk as handcarts and all three of them had a bottle of vodka in each hand insisting that we drank with them so out came our enamel mugs; they drank out of the bottles.

They were over the moon about something and after a lot of sign language and looking at our maps we found out what it was all about.

The Russians were making a stand at Stalingrad and Grozny. It looked as if we had had a lucky escape and besides that we heard on the BBC news that our lot were holding the front at El Alamein and that the Yanks in England were drinking all the beer and shagging all the girls by way of celebration.

Two days later we got the order to return to Tehran.

Before getting well up into the mountains I decided that we should stay the night in the forest where it would be warmer and that by the next night we would be well down the other side.

The trouble was that as Robbie Burns once said, 'the best laid plans of mice and men often go awry' or something like that, and he knew what he was talking about.

After getting settled down in a clearing at the side of the road and having our gourmet meal of stew with a packet of biscuits it was into our bunks, the usual chatter and off to sleep.

I didn't bother to put a guard on; Harry the driver thought that I should. He had gone off bears now and kept going on about werewolves.

The next morning as we got higher up the mountain it was much colder and going through the tunnel there were workmen on scaffolding chopping down icicles that hung down from the roof of the tunnel like stalactites.

When we arrived at the place where we camped on our way up I decided we should pull in and spend the night there again and maybe make it back to Tehran the next day.

There had been a fall of snow that had melted and left the ground in a muddy state.

That night the frost came and could we hell as like move the wagon the next morning. In the toolbox we had a pick, shovel and a machete but they were no use. The tyres were well and truly stuck. Every time Harry tried to move the wagon it looked as if the tyres were going to be ripped off. We tried boiling water, not knowing at the time that boiling water freezes quicker than cold water.

One good thing was that he had remembered to drain the radiator the night before.

Yoddy sent a message to our headquarters telling them we were frozen in. After a while he got a brief reply saying 'Do your best.'

I decided that the best thing to do was get plenty of fuel in before more snow came, so off I went with Archie and Harry to where there were some small clusters of pine trees. We took the machete to do the chopping and a rope to tie the branches into bundles and lower them down the mountain to the camp.

Harry was holding a branch back and I was doing the chopping. As I was swinging the machete back to make a chop it came to a sudden stop. I had caught him right in the middle of the forehead with the point of the machete.

The blood was streaming down his face and dripping off his chin end, with four letter words going non-stop all ending up with the word idiot coming through the blood. Meanwhile Archie was struggling to get his field dressing out of his pocket. In our trousers there was a pocket specially made to carry a field dressing which was made up of a pad of layers of lint with a bandage attached and it came in very handy at times like this.

We got Harry down to the wagon and cleaned his head up. By now it had stopped bleeding. It was a deep gash about two inches long and after he had calmed down he volunteered to have it stitched up.

In the first aid box there were some sterilised needles and catgut and off I went on my first sewing lesson. Yoddy held the skin together and I got the first stitch in and tied it.

Archie, who was looking on, suggested I did what he called chain stitch, which I tried and found to be much better. I think the pain in Harry's head was worse than the pain of the needle so he didn't notice it.

Fortunately, Taffy Hughes turned up the next day with the ration wagon so we were able to get poor old Harry and Ralph Needham back to base. Ralph was a nice enough lad but not cut out for roughing it. At the beginning in Iraq when we had sorted ourselves out into posts, Andy our CO had said that any lad that got fed up could always pack it in and go back to base.

Two days later Smithy the Cockney and my old pal Frank Routledge turned up on a Russian wagon as replacements; they had hitch-hiked from Tehran.

We were only at this spot for about two weeks but with all that happened in that time it seemed more like two years.

The day after Frank and Smithy arrived we had visitors. Two men came from the village down the road, one of them was crying. His name was Fatala and the man with him was the village hunter, his name was Gadam Ali.

It took us a while to fathom out what the trouble was with us not speaking Persian and them not speaking English. In fact I don't think most of the people in that part of the world had ever seen any Europeans before.

After a lot of sign language we found that there had been an accident and that they wanted us to go with them and see what we could do.

Yoddy and I went along with them.

Fatala's son, Asala, a boy about six years old, had been taking some sheep up the mountain when one of them had dislodged a stone and it fell down onto his head.

When I saw his head it made Harry's accident look like a scratch.

Yoddy went back to the wagon for the first aid kit.

In the meantime one of the women of the house had got a bowl of hot water ready as I thought that the first thing that I would have to do was to get the wound cleaned up.

Whilst waiting for Yoddy to return I naturally had a look at the house, it had only one room.

There were shelves on the walls with hens perched on them. In one corner was a barrel with a live turkey in it, presumably getting fattened up for some celebration or other.

The thing that fascinated me the most was the table. It was in the centre of the room and in the middle of the table was a hole about two feet in diameter, down the hole was a grate with a charcoal fire in it. On the table there was a cover with about three foot of eiderdown sewn round the edge of it.

The idea was that when they had eaten their evening meal they would all snuggle down with their legs under the table and their feet near the fire, pull the eiderdown over themselves and go to sleep.

Hence the saying: 'One half of the world doesn't know how the other half lives, or sleeps in some cases.'

I found out later that it is called a coursee. When we had the boy's head cleaned up it looked as if a sharp corner of the stone had struck his skull. It hadn't cracked it but there was a small hole; where the bit of bone from the hole had gone we never found out.

Yoddy trotted back to the wagon again to get a razor to shave the boy's head around the wound.

When he had gone I began wondering what to do about the hole and it came to my mind that sometime in the past I had read in a book or seen in a film something about inserting a thin piece of silver.

When Yoddy came back we talked it over and he said that it

didn't matter much what we did as the boy would most likely die anyway. As the boy was still unconscious he couldn't feel any pain which was just as well.

Back to the wagon again; a five rili coin; made it red hot and, using the head of the pick as an anvil, beat it out thin enough to make it pliable, and then back down to Fatala's house.

Using the blade from the razor I cut the skin, peeled it back then brought it forward over the metal what was covering the hole.

Stitching the skin together over the hole was a tricky job as the skin had shrunk a bit, it was more darning than sewing. Plenty of iodine and a field dressing on it and all we could do now was hope for the best.

The comical part of all this was that on our course at St. Athan the only first aid they taught us was how to apply a tourniquet and make splints. Two days later Asala regained consciousness; he had lost use of one of his arms but I can't remember which one.

I remember telling his mother in sign language to feed him on eggs mixed with goat's milk. I wonder where I had picked that tip up.

The news of our medical skills must have flown around the villages for it was only the day after when two men turned up with a young woman perched on the back of a mule. Her right leg was fastened up in a kind of a sling suspended from the mule's neck.

The men kept pointing at her leg and saying 'Konoon por.' I found out later that Konoon was Persian for woman and that por was leg and what a mess that leg was.

The dressing they had put on was a piece of red flannel and on removing it the sight was enough to make me sick. The bottom end of her leg was so swollen that her foot and her leg looked to be all one. It was all colours and the open wound on her calf was all crusted with dried blood and yellow pus. Harry Clark said that it looked like gangrene and going by the stink it could well have been. Not that I had ever seen or smelled gangrene before but I had heard old soldiers from the First World War talk about it.

The two men came every day with the mule to take Yoddy and me to tend the leg.

All we could think of doing was putting bread poultices on it; the amount of stuff that came out of the leg was amazing, that barley bread of theirs must have had marvellous drawing power.

After four or five days the leg was down to normal and all that was left were the open wounds where the fangs of some vicious animal had gone in.

How we did all this with our limited knowledge of such things I will never know. I think it was more luck than management.

Every day we got a good meal of rice and lamb, or fish fresh from the river and a chicken and half a dozen eggs to take back to the lads.

The village hunter Gadam Ali had a very old gun that looked like it had been used at the Battle of Waterloo. He poured powder into the breach and pushed the ball down the barrel wrapped in a bit of rag. When he went up the mountain hunting deer his success wasn't what you would call one hundred per cent. When he saw our rifles his eyes lit up so I lent him mine and off he went up the mountain with his two pals. They came back with two lovely young deer or gazelle; I could never tell the difference. They took them down to the village, skinned them and brought us back four of the best cuts.

Harry Clark, who had been a butcher, said that it was too fresh to eat but we did and it was a treat.

We seemed to be settling down in our mountain retreat and although it was very cold we kept a good fire going and slept in our clothes.

A week or two previously a Russian convoy going north saw that we were having trouble with the ice. The officer in the leading wagon, who spoke fluent English, said that on their way back if we were still frozen in they would have a go at getting us out.

They arrived back as promised and were well prepared; they had brought a big bag of salt with them. It didn't take long to get us free.

Whilst celebrating our freedom with a tot or two of vodka I could hear Archie telling the officer that he was a member of the Communist party in Glasgow. The officer was going on about getting rid of the capitalists in Britain after the war and becoming allies of Russia. It makes me think now about the plans of mice and men again.

As we were freeing the wagon a droll-looking chap came along riding on a mule with a donkey following on behind carrying what looked like all his worldly goods on its sides in about half a dozen carpet bags. He was well turned out in a large fur overcoat, riding boots and a flat cap with earflaps.

After the usual greetings of 'Salam-Alekum' etc. he asked who the doctor was that had tended to the boy in the village. He spoke good English.

Yoddy pointed at me and I pointed at Yoddy. It seemed to puzzle him, having two doctors between the six of us.

It turned out that he was the doctor for that area and that he set out from Tehran every three months and visited all the villages in the mountains.

On explaining to him that we weren't doctors and that we had done what we thought was best, he congratulated us on what a good job we had done.

With that bit of praise going to my head I told him about the woman with the leg, it made him laugh when I called her Konoon Por.

Things were happening at last. After the doctor and Russian had gone I got the codebook out and sent a message to headquarters saying that we were returning to base.

Next morning we set off early. We got there late the same day and found that ours was the last post to arrive. It looked as if they had been waiting for us, as they were ready for moving off.

The following day, bright and early, we headed west to a place called Kazvin and made camp for the night just outside the town.

One place that I will always remember was Kermanshah. The night that we stayed there, after having our evening meal of stew and biscuits, a few of us strolled into the town to have a look round and stretch our legs.

In the suq (market) the stalls were illuminated by oil lamps and lots of them were selling fur coats, gloves and caps, all made from cat skins. It made me wonder what happened to the cats and I couldn't stop thinking about the Maconochie stew.

We soon got tired of wandering about and there was nowhere we could get a drink, not of alcohol anyway, and that was all we were interested in. Except Archie who got himself a little stock of opium from one of the coffee shops.

It seemed strange that you could go into a coffee shop and get a pipe of opium and a sniff of cocaine but alcohol was strictly forbidden.

The next morning we were in the mountains again and going through the Kermanshah Pass. Some of the lads who had the misfortune to be riding in the back of the wagons were complaining about the cold. If they pulled the flaps down they were choked by the fumes, if they had the flaps up it was enough to freeze your bollocks off so we took it in turns riding in front with the driver, one on the seat and one on the engine box.

Whilst we were all moaning about the cold, a convoy of Indian troops was heading the other way. They had no windscreens in their vehicles, just a piece of canvas that came up to the tips of their noses.

They were Gurkhas on their way overland to India and then most likely on to Burma. They had just done eighteen months in action in the Western Desert.

Out of the mountains and onto the desert once again we arrived at the border between Iran and Iraq at a place called Kanakin. It was about midday so the convoy had pulled up for an hour while we had our tiffin which was, as usual, half a tin of corned beef, a packet of biscuits and a mug of tea. Now that we were in Iraq again we could start looking forward to a packet of dates for pudding.

On the side of the road, squatted behind their little tables, were the money exchangers haggling about changing our rils into fils.

It was much warmer now and although it was bumpy and dusty it was more pleasant than the cold.

Iran didn't strike me as being a very pleasant place. The only time that we had been able to have a bath was at the silk factory by the Caspian Sea; since then we had never taken our clothes off because of the cold, hence some little friends had joined us in the shape of lice.

There were three kinds of lice known to us at the time; these were head lice, body lice and crabs. Trying to get rid of them is a futile task: we tried powder and solutions that were supposed to do the trick with no success. Someone came up with an idea that they used in the First World War about burning the seams of our clothes over a lighted candle. It didn't work.

It was a long time before we won the battle against them and when we did it was so simple and hilarious.

Baghdad hadn't changed much since our last visit; on we went over the rivers and on to Fallujah finishing up once again at the transit camp at Habbaniyah.

The last time we had been at the camp the CO had asked Wilson (the lad taken onto the ship in handcuffs) if he would like to stay at the transit camp on cookhouse duties as they were short handed. Wilson volunteered as it was a way of getting more food. The CO had been glad to get him off the unit as he was still a bit of a rebel.

Lo and behold, Wilson had gone up in the world and was now the sergeant in charge of the cookhouse.

It crossed my mind immediately that now was my chance for second helpings at meal times in repayment for the cigs and chocolate that I had passed through the bars to him when he was in the cell on the *Duchess of Richmond*. His immediate reply was, 'No, you always were a greedy bastard.' It was then I stopped believing in one good turn deserving another.

The first day that we were at the transit camp our CO went across to the main camp to ask if we could have use of their showers.

When he came back he got us all on parade to tell us that we could not only have use of the showers but also the cinema, swimming pool and the NAAFI. To put icing on the cake, I received a pack of letters from home. There was a lot from Jean, one from my dad and one from my brother Harry telling me what a rotten time he was having in the army now he had been posted from Sheffield to bonny Scotland.

Good things never seem to last for long. Our stay at Habbaniyah only lasted three more days. We didn't know at the time that there was a rush to get all the spare troops across to Egypt for the final advance in the Western Desert and North Africa.

One day in the NAAFI I got talking to some lads that had been at Habbaniyah for nearly two years. They told me that the airfield had been attacked the year before by an army of pro-nazi Arabs led by a chap called Rashid Ali.

They were shelling the camp from a plateau about a mile away and were ready for storming the camp when, in the nick of time, a battalion of British infantry arrived, causing Rashid and his merry men to beat a hasty retreat. He made his last stand at a place called Fort Rutba and from there disappeared into the blue.

If you care to look up the history of Iraq you will find there has been fighting between the tribes going on for thousands of years even before they discovered the oil.

It seemed strange to me that the men at the top were rushing troops from west to east to the Burma campaign and rushing others east to west to Egypt but, ours is not to reason why when there are clever people paid to do our reasoning for us. Anyway I would sooner be going west than east as it got us nearer home and in the desert you could usually see what was going on. Not like in the jungle where the Japanese bastards would be sniping at you from behind the trees and then cutting your balls off for good measure.

We were now on our way to Egypt. The journey was uneventful.

The convoy did about one hundred and twenty miles, which does not seem much these days but having governors on the wagons, for some reason I could never understand, meant that the vehicles could only do about twenty miles an hour across the rough desert tracks.

One night we made camp on the outskirts of Amman, the capital of Jordan and a few of us went to the local cinema.

The next day we came to the Jordan valley which has always been a puzzle to me. As we descended the road into the valley there were sign posts indicating how far you were below sea level. At its lowest point it was thirteen hundred feet below sea level. What mystified me at the time was why the valley didn't fill up with water as I had always believed that water always finds its own level. I have had it explained to me since but even now it still seems a bit of a mystery.

On and on we went, bypassing Jerusalem, heading south to Gaza, then to Bea-Sheba and turning west to cross the Sinai desert. We were now in Lawrence of Arabia country.

10
Egypt

After crossing the Sinai we arrived at the ferry at Ismailia on the Suez Canal. It was a small ferry working on a chain and cogwheel principle with an Arab lethargically winding the handle. Not that you could blame him as he would be on about twenty pence a day with no prospects. It took nearly all day to get the whole of our unit across leaving a long queue behind us.

It was now a nice tarmac road all the way to Cairo with army camps on each side of the road for most of the way. On passing the Sweet Water Canal the stink was overpowering; it wasn't long before I found out the whole of Egypt had the same smell. I suspect that it will be much different now with all the tourism that's going on there.

About twenty miles up the River Nile from Cairo is a town called Helwan; we stayed at a transit camp there on the outskirts of the town servicing the wagons and replenishing our stores etc. A constant guard had to be kept as thieving was the main industry in Egypt in those days.

There was a sense of urgency everywhere and after three or four days we were on our way through Cairo and up the road to the coast.

I had no idea until then how much equipment was needed to fight a major battle; on each side of the road for most of the way were wagons, tanks, guns, thousands of shells and everything else you could think of. All this was in reserve to replace losses in the battle zone.

I had heard it said that General Montgomery would not launch the final assault until he was certain of victory and by the look of things he knew what he was talking about.

11
North Africa

* * * * * * * *

The desert is dead
Everything dies in the desert
First hope dies
Then faith dies
Then youth lays dead
With all the young men
In the desert

J.D.

* * * * * * * *

It was a long time before we actually became operational so we travelled on up the coast road from El Alamein and past places that have become well known through films and books since the Second World War. Places like Mersa Matru, Sidi Barani, Halfaya Pass etc.

The carnage and destruction was unbelievable. Tanks, guns, vehicles of all shapes and sizes and all the other stuff warmongers produce for common soldiers to slaughter each other with.

There were South African non-combatant Negroes digging up bodies from where they had fallen in battle and taking them back to be put in communal graves and later transferred into the massive military cemeteries at El Alamein. I was beginning to find that life is the cheapest commodity in the world.

On and on through Egypt, Cyrenaicia and Libya with the

stench of death everywhere.

At Leptis Magna the unit became operational at last. Our post was given a map reference about fifty miles south-southwest which took us well into the desert and more or less to the front line. The majority of the soldiers we passed on the way were New Zealanders.

We set up our stall in a little wadi out of sight of the enemy. Smithie and I went to the top of the wadi bank with the field telephone, dug a trench and there we were, ready for action.

There wasn't much going on during the day except for a few tanks moving about in the distance and the occasional sound of gunfire. What did keep us busy was our aircraft going over to bomb the enemy lines. Some bright spark had had the idea of fixing a Bofors cannon underneath the fuselage of some Hurricane fighters that went in at almost ground level firing at tanks. The results proved to be very effective.

During the night engineers and infantry would go forward clearing lanes in the mine fields so tanks could go through at first light.

After two days we received a message ordering us to move twenty miles south and after a while turn northwest towards Tripoli.

Christmas came and went without us noticing.

There was a lot of hard fighting going on and although the Germans and Italians were retreating they were still making a stand wherever they could. The little information we received came from gossip passed onto us by army lads.

On the 23rd of January we were back on the coast at our headquarters and passing through Tripoli which had fallen during the night.

The unit carried on slowly along the coast road going through Zavia and Sabratha until we came to a little town called Zuara where we made camp and the headquarters staff got settled in among the palm trees at the top of the beach. Although the town was bombed and battered it struck me what a lovely place it would have been in peacetime.

Another day or two and we were on our way again south into the desert to carry on observing. The first position we took up was near a French Foreign Legion post called Fort Isria.

Just before nightfall, after we had dug in and got the wireless fixed up for our six o'clock collective call, the field telephone rang. It was Archie on watch in the trench at the top of the rise he was 'specking out' from. He said there was a vehicle approaching from a westerly direction in a cloud of dust. I decided to let it get closer, hoping if it was the enemy they would pass by without seeing us and if they did see us they would be near enough for us to open fire and take them by surprise.

Lady Luck was on our side; it turned out to be a captain and two privates from the Foreign Legion.

I went to the top of the rise and waved to them. They came over in their fifteen hundredweight truck. The captain got out and walked towards us. As he approached us I told Archie to do the talking as he spoke French fluently. The captain heard me and in broad Yorkshire asked, 'What part of Yorkshire do you come from?' He was from Ripon and had been in the Legion for fourteen years so it was time for a chat and a brew.

We had a good laugh when he told us that the two men with him were Germans. The French Foreign Legion took men of any nationality; many of them were ex-jailbirds.

The next morning he brought us four big bottles of wine, it tasted like vinegar but we drank it.

There was an oasis near the fort so we filled our mule tanks and got busy with the Bell steriliser.

Our rations were getting smaller every time Taffy Hughes came to drop them off but the letters from home were getting more consistent and Jean was writing about twice a week. They were still taking about three months to reach us but, when you think about it, it seemed a great feat of organisation to get rations, letters and everything else to hundreds of thousands of troops when the enemy still held the upper hand in the Med.

Every time the letters came I expected to get one from Jean saying she had met someone else. Sometimes I thought she might have done and didn't want to upset me.

All of us had lost weight; I estimated I had lost one and a half stone in about twelve months. We still had our lice to contend with and we had all got desert sores on our arms and legs, still, there's nothing like a good moan for keeping you happy.

One morning after Yoddy had finished his shift on the wireless he wandered off into the desert without say a word to anyone, I thought that he must have been feeling down in the dumps and wanted some time to himself.

It was the middle of the afternoon when he got back looking a bit guilty, he got me away from the others and confessed to me that he had taken a tin of jam out of the ration box and eaten it.

It was the only tin we had and we'd been saving it for the day when we might get some bread.

At first I felt mad and it crossed my mind to send him back to base and then I felt sorry and told him it might never be missed by the others.

Later on, he told the others what he had done, nobody said anything they just sat there looking sad.

Looking on the bright side we were now getting one bottle of beer each a week and fifty 'V' cigarettes; three of us didn't smoke so the other three had a hundred each to keep them happy. Frank didn't drink but he thought that one bottle a week wouldn't do his boxing career any harm. He didn't realise that it would be old age that would be his knockout.

For a while now we had been moving around the eastern side of a big salt lake in southern Tunisia.

The news from the army lads we met on our way was that the Germans had repulsed an attack by the Americans at a place called Kasserine and that thousands of Yanks had been killed.

We kept on going towards a town called Gafsa with the enemy on our right who looked to be going in the same direction as ourselves. It wasn't any use us trying to work it out so we just kept moving on and sending our messages.

One morning we settled in on a piece of hollow ground by a rocky outcrop. There was a dugout ready made for our observation post; I inspected it for booby traps and found a Life Magazine that was very popular in America at the time.

Smithie was the first to pick it up but he only looked at the pictures. Archie got hold of it next and was having a good read when all of a sudden he said, 'Have a look at this, Gun.' He passed me the magazine and there it was in black and white. The life cycle of a louse.

On reading the article I found that they lay their eggs on the hairs under your arms and any other parts of the body where hairs happen to grow, after three weeks the eggs hatch out and the mammy and daddy lice die or fade away or something.

This information set us thinking and Harry Clark came up with the idea that if we shaved off all our body hairs and wore nothing but our PT shorts for three weeks and a bit it might do the trick.

Everything went fine as we shaved under our arms and around our private parts but when it came to round our arseholes it became a bit of a problem and we realised that the only way to do it was to shave each others; so it was a matter of choose your partners.

Yoddy and I got paired up and to show a good example we got cracking. At first it was what you could call embarrassing but we had made our minds up that our nasty little friends had to go.

After a while it became hilarious. Frank got a photograph of Archie shaving Smithie with his spectacles perched on the end of his nose looking like a university professor. I have often wondered if he kept it, if he could get anyone to develop and print it.

Three weeks went by and there wasn't a louse in sight except for some American Air Force clowns who strafed us with machine gun fire for three mornings on the run. This was what is now termed as 'friendly fire' and they are still at it. It must be handed down from one generation to the next.

Having now passed Gafsa we continued in a north-westerly direction towards the southern end of the Mareth Line; a defence line built by the Germans and Italians while occupying Tunisia.

It was now well into the month of March and feeling much warmer.

One morning I happened to be washing and dressing my desert sores when an Arab came along wanting to exchange eggs for packets of biscuits which was a long drawn out task as we had to haggle for each egg separately.

He was alarmed when he saw me washing the sores. With a bit of a language struggle he insisted that we should keep them dry without a dressing and let the flies get at them and they would eat the badness out. We tried it and it worked.

It seems strange that the Arabs knew this all those years ago and that now it is common practice in our hospitals to use maggots for similar problems.

When we came to a house, which was quite often now as we were leaving the desert behind and finding the land more fertile and cultivated, the first thing we did was to search for booby traps and, if there was a cellar, throw a hand grenade down the cellar steps just to make sure that they hadn't left a trap of some kind down there.

Frank didn't like the idea as he argued that there might be German or Italian soldiers hiding there.

My argument was that if one of us went down to have a look there may be someone down there with an itchy trigger finger pointing a rifle at you, but no matter what I said he didn't like it.

One evening we got a message on the collective call to proceed to a position only about five miles away so I decided to stay where we were then pack up and move off at first light the following morning.

On arriving at the map reference we saw that there was a small farmhouse about three hundred yards away so we decided to set our observation post up on the roof and to sleep in the house which to all intents and purpose was unoccupied. It looked as if it had been someone's pride and joy before the war. There was a nice little olive grove of about two acres, a little vineyard and a vegetable garden. There were no poultry or animals as they would have been taken for the pot by the troops.

A windmill pumped water from underground into a concrete tank with a sluice gate for irrigating the land.

None of it had been sabotaged so it looked as if it had been bypassed by the enemy.

Little did I know at the time that this was the day that would haunt me for the rest of my life.

We did our usual search for booby traps and found none. We didn't look in the cellar and as normal I went to the wagon and got a hand grenade out of the box.

As I was about to pull the pin out Frank said, 'Don't do it, Gun.'

He was too late and out came the pin that releases the lever as soon as the grenade leaves your grip and explodes four seconds later.

The cellar steps went down so far then there was a wall and a turn to the right with a few more steps continuing down into the cellar. I threw the grenade so that it would ricochet off the wall and go into the cellar which it did.

I turned and ran out of the house followed by an almighty blast and clouds of dust.

After the dust had settled Archie said, 'Who's going down to have a look?'

Smithie said, ‘Gun threw it so I vote that he goes down.’ No one made a move so off I went. There was a wire grille high up on the back wall of the cellar and when I saw it I thought that what I should have done was looked round at the back of the house and I would have saved a grenade as the grille would have been letting in enough light to see by.

I sat on the bottom step waiting for the dust to settle and when it did I felt sick at first. There across the cellar, sat on the floor with their backs against the wall, was a woman with one arm round a little boy and her other arm round a girl.

It’s funny how one’s mind works at times like this. As I sat there feeling nauseated and shivering all over I thought of when I was about four years old and my mother sat on the couch in front of the fire with her arm around me on one side and my sister on the other giving us a cuddle. It was then that I started to cry and I have never cried since.

After a while Smithie shouted down. ‘What are you doing, Gun? Have you found yourself a bint?’

I staggered up the steps wondering if it was all a dream and I would waken up and everything would be fine. But as soon as I walked out into the sunlight I could tell by the look on their faces on seeing my face they knew that something horrible had happened.

Nobody spoke at first, then Frank went into the house and down the cellar steps. After a couple of minutes he came out of the house, took one look at me and said, ‘You bastard Gun.’

It was the last time that Frank spoke to me except for in the line of duty. I had lost my closest friend.

Smithie was the next to go and have a look, on coming up he said in his Cockney twang, ‘Do you realise, Cpl. Davidson, that you have committed an act of murder.’ He sounded like a high court judge.

The others went down one at a time. Archie said that it wasn’t our fault, it was the doings of the capitalists who make their millions out of making armaments so that ignorant people like us could kill each other just to keep them in the lap of luxury. Harry put the blame on power mad people like Hitler.

Yoddy didn’t say anything.

We didn’t set our post up in the house. The next day we got the order to move on.

A day or two after I was not feeling much better when I remembered that we hadn't had the decency or the guts to bury the bodies.

As we made our way towards the coast things were not the same. There were not the stories at night when we sat around the fire. Frank did not go on any more about his dreams of what he would do after the war, of building houses and owning a dance hall. It was all a long way off but there was no harm in dreaming and things were getting better. It looked as if we had won in North Africa and that was our second victory after the Battle of Britain.

At last we reached the coast just outside the town of Sfax where headquarters had set up camp. We were all together once more and being by the sea enabled us to wash the sand off our bodies.

We had a walk into the town and found that it had been heavily bombed by the Americans who had been trying to bomb the docks and had managed to hit almost everything except the docks. This caused a lot of unrest with the civilians who lived there.

What amazed me most of all were the amount of prisoners that the infantry and the military police were bringing along the coast road who all had to be fed and watered.

Most of them were Italian. I found out from one Italian who spoke perfect English that the reason they were giving themselves up in such large numbers was that they had come to the conclusion that if Germany won the war they would be taken over by Hitler and the Nazis and Italy would cease to exist. But if the Allies won they would be allowed to carry on as an independent country. It wasn't long after this that Italy saw the light and capitulated.

We had a laugh one day when we saw an infantryman coming along the road; he was about five foot four in height leading about a hundred big German lads of the Africa Korps down the road. They looked dumbfounded, the little Tommy had his tin hat at a jaunty angle, his rifle slung over his shoulder and a big smile on his face. For our benefit as he went past he turned round and shouted, 'Come on you big silly buggers.'

We were not at Sfax for long when we packed up and set off along the coast back to Libya.

There were plenty of rumours as to where we would be going

next. The commonest one was that we would be going on an invasion of Sicily.

Lady Luck was with us again and the rumours were wrong.

Not far over the Libyan border there was a fort called Fort Tempesta where we got our heads down for the night.

The next morning the CO had us on parade and informed us that we were going to be on coast patrol. The beach was about half a mile down a track from the fort and our post was at the bottom of the track. The idea was that the enemy might still have a go at landing troops and causing bother.

We set our little camp up at the top of the beach in the sand dunes and all we had to do was patrol a mile each way from our post reporting any aircraft or ships that were about and keeping our eyes open for an invasion which seemed very unlikely, for from what I had seen I thought that the German and Italian soldiers were glad to be out of North Africa once and for all and looking forward to their sausages and spaghetti.

I found it very pleasant just strolling along the beach for two hours out of every six and having a dip in the sea whenever I felt like it.

Sometimes Harry or Yoddy would go with me for a bit of exercise as it only needed one on the transmitter.

Frank stayed back at the fort as we didn't need a driver and I don't think that he was keen on my company any more. I felt sorry about that for if I had taken any notice of him at the farmhouse in Tunisia everything would have carried on as usual.

The trouble is that hindsight never altered anything but sometimes it stops you from making the same mistake again.

One morning, when Yoddy and I were strolling along the beach, we saw a body at the water's edge. All he had on was a pair of khaki shorts. His face didn't look so good as half of his chin on the right hand side was missing. His right arm and hand were in a sorry state and his chest was split open.

Yoddy went back to the tent for a spade and I looked for a spot to bury him. There was nobody about except for an Arab boy a hundred yards away looking after some goats.

Yoddy came back with the spade and we dug a shallow grave at the top of the beach, dropped him in and filled it up; we presumed he was off a ship that had been sunk and he had been washed ashore.

At tiffin time, when we were sat having our bully beef and biscuits, I asked Harry to enter it in the log book as he was the duty wireless operator at the time. Yoddy said, 'He couldn't have been in the sea for long as he was still bleeding.'

No one spoke for a few seconds as we all realised that dead bodies don't bleed.

Archie was the first to break the silence by saying in his broad Glasgow twang, 'Well there's no doubt he's dead the noo.'

The next morning along came an Arab who somehow knew about the burial on the beach; it must have been the little Arab boy with his goats.

Archie and I went along to the grave with the man who thought that it may be his uncle.

We scraped the sand off his face but no, it wasn't his uncle.

The next day two more Arabs came claiming that it may be their brother who had gone fishing with little bombs that they made from gelignite bound in a rag, a detonator and a bit of greasy string for a fuse. (There was plenty such stuff lying about for making such things.) The idea was to see a shoal of fish in a breaker, light the fuse and throw the bomb at the shoal. And it usually worked but not for this unfortunate fisherman, he held it too long. It was their brother and amidst their tears, wailing and moaning they said they would come back later and take him away for a proper funeral.

The family did come back later with what seemed to be half the population of Libya with them.

They dug the body up and wrapped it in white sheets and draped it on a donkey. All the time this was going on the ladies stood around making that funny noise with their tongues which seemed to be the custom on sad occasions.

The old man of the family kept coming over to me and didn't seem pleased at all with how Yoddy and I had handled the first burial. After a while with my little knowledge of Arabic and a lot of sign language I gathered the complaints were that we hadn't buried him with his head towards Mecca. I wondered what would have happened if they had known that he wasn't dead. The only consolation for me was that, had he miraculously survived, I don't think he would have enjoyed his fishing any more.

It had been very pleasant living by the sea for a few weeks and on two occasions we got a loaf of white bread in our rations.

Things like that seem so trivial now but at the time it was such a treat that it is still in my memory to this day.

Once again the unit got the order to move, so off we went along the coast road towards Tripoli and at Zuara we camped for three or four days among the palm trees at the top of the beach.

One day while looking around in what was left of the church I found a box with some tubes of oil colours in it, a bottle of turpentine and a couple of brushes; I suspected that an Italian soldier had left them behind.

When the next batch of letters came there was one from Jean with a photograph in it.

I cut a piece of cardboard off one of the ration boxes and took it to Ginger Mason, the corporal in charge of the main stores, to see if he had some white paint to prime my piece of cardboard with. After giving it a couple of coats of paint I got cracking and painted a copy of the photograph; I still have the photo and the copy. It isn't a good copy but I have kept it all those years.

The next place we stopped at along the coast was a little town called Sabratha. Most of the houses in the town were deserted so there were plenty of places to sleep.

I could have got a bit bored by the unit not being operational as there wasn't much to do.

In between the town and the beach there were the fantastic remains of a Roman city. Even though I had seen some of the wonders of the world such as the Hanging Gardens of Babylon, the Pharaoh's Lighthouse, the Sphinx and the Pyramids I had not been really interested until now. So I was anything but bored and spent most of my time admiring the skill and ingenuity of the ancient Romans.

There was a caretaker on the site and when he saw how interested I was he explained lots of things about the place to me. He told me that in its heyday there had once been a harbour where now were just the remains of a mole or breakwater jutting out into the sea.

The Romans, or more likely the slaves, brought lions all the way from the African jungle and across the Sahara desert to Sabratha and then shipped them to Rome to be used in the Coliseum for the Romans' Saturday nights out. There were frescoes on walls and friezes with the colours as fresh now as when first painted onto the wet plaster; a magnificent thirty seat public lavatory, a theatre where the back of the stage was the façade of an elaborate building.

These were just a few of the things that made my mind boggle and besides that, I think it was the forerunner of the little education I have acquired since.

One day when I was strolling along the beach I saw Ginger Mason hard at work digging into a bank of sand eight or nine feet high at the top of the beach. I went to see what he was up to.

There he was with a pick and shovel, a sieve and a logbook; he put me in mind of the gold prospectors I had seen in the cowboy films.

When he saw I was interested he said, 'I expect you want to know what I'm doing?'

I did and he told me that he was looking for Roman artefacts. I didn't know what artefacts were but not wanting to show my ignorance I didn't say so.

He said that I could help him so long as I didn't tell anyone if we found anything. I doubted if we would find anything after all these years but I had nothing else to do so I thought that it would pass on an hour or two.

I dug with the pick and shovel and he made busy with the sieve.

We hadn't been at it long before he got all excited and shouted, 'Look at this.' It was a round, grubby looking piece of metal and when he had cleaned it up I saw it was a coin of some kind. To me it looked like a badly made old penny.

After he got over his excitement he entered it in his logbook and I noticed that there were a lot of previous entries and it made me wonder if he was an old hand at the game and had been doing a bit of digging in other places of antiquity we had called at on our travels.

On most afternoons during our stop at Sabratha I went to help him and all the bits and pieces we found he entered in his book.

I never told any of the lads at the time that we had found anything so all they did was laugh at me and say that we were wasting our time. Even so it was better than lying in your pit all day thinking of England.

One afternoon I was digging away and shovelling the sand into the sieve when Ginger went red in the face and was shouting over and over again, 'Look at this!' At first I had no idea what it was.

After he had cleaned it up I saw it was a little metal figure. He told me it was gold and was called an amulet. He let me hold it and I had never realised before how heavy gold was.

Ginger always seemed to be worrying about keeping his finds secret. Now I know why. I found out years later there was a British Officer in charge of antiquities and with his counterpart in the German army they made arrangements about historical sites not being damaged during the fighting, making sure that they were bypassed and nothing was taken away.

It was no wonder Ginger had me sworn to secrecy.

The officer in charge at the time was the late Sir Mortimer Wheeler who became well known in later years on TV as a historian.

This lull in the unit's activities came to an end and in a while we were off again along the road. Near a small town called Zavia, about thirty miles west of Tripoli, we were on coast patrol again.

Our headquarters set their camp up on the outskirts of the town and we made our way to a map reference about two miles to the west near the coast. Nearby was a deserted farmhouse where we fixed up our post and got settled in.

The farmhouse had the usual sign painted on the wall in large block letters. Colonisation Della Libiya.

This Colonisation business had been one of Mussolini's better ideas. In Italy in the nineteen thirties there was a lot of unemployment like everywhere else so he had this idea of building small farms on the coast of Libya, which at that time belonged to Italy, and invited families to go and occupy them.

Whatever they produced after the first year or two they kept a percentage for themselves to live on and handed the rest over to the warehouse in the local town.

We had only been there a few days when an Italian chap turned up from out of nowhere. He was wearing a trilby hat, a blue cotton shirt, khaki drill trousers and a pair of Italian army desert boots.

He spoke good English and told us that his father had lived in America for twenty years and now his father and the family had a restaurant in a small town called Aquila near Rome.

I don't know where he slept but he would turn up each morning and have a brew and a chat. Some days he would bring eggs and flour, from where I don't know but it was always welcome. One day he taught us how to make spaghetti and that I have never forgotten.

Smithie insisted that he was one of the types that we had to look out for on our coast patrol caper.

After a while he took us into his confidence and told us his story. His name was Jan Rossetti and he had been a sergeant in the regular army. He had been left behind in the retreat and was given shelter by some Bedouins. He didn't say where he had got his civvy clothes.

I was at a loss what to do with him. I knew that I should have handed him over as a prisoner of war so we took a vote on it. There was only Smithie that voted that we should hand him over so that was settled.

About half a mile away was another farm with a big camp of Negro soldiers nearby from Djibouti who had French officers. One evening I had a walk over to the other farm and found that it was a brothel catering for the Djibouti lads.

The Madam made me welcome and I sat at the table in the middle of the room and had a cup of coffee with her.

There were four girls, two Italians and two Arabs.

Whilst the Madam and I were drinking our coffee and having a chat the girls were sat, one in each corner of the room, on what looked to me like witches' cauldrons like those you see in children's books. Underneath each of the cauldrons was a little charcoal fire.

The Madam saw me looking at the set up and tried to explain to me in half English and half Italian that in the cauldrons was water with alum in and the steam coming from it tightened the girls 'working parts' up for the next day's work.

In the next room were four cubicles with blankets draped across the entrances.

As I was leaving she asked me if I would like to join her for supper the following evening. I asked her if I could bring one of the other lads with me as I thought when I told them about the alum pots they would never believe me. She said I could as long as he behaved himself and that we would be having spaghetti with cheese and tomato.

The Madam and I became good friends and my visits became a regular thing and furthered my education considerably. One evening after supper we were having our little chat, the girls were sat on the pots lost in clouds of steam and she got round to explaining to me the financial side of the business.

Each of the four girls was entertaining between fifteen and twenty clients a day at ten shillings (50p) a go. This was split fifty-fifty between her and the girls which made it five bob each, so at four times fifteen times five bob, Madam was raking in about fifteen pounds a day; quite a sum in those days. Her only overhead was food and I gathered most of it came from the French Quartermaster's store for favours received.

She had her future all worked out if every thing went according to plan. I hope it did for she seemed a kind lady and I think she had taken a liking to me in a motherly kind of way as I was only young and she would be in her mid-forties which seemed really old to me at the time.

Her plan was that if the Germans and Italians won the war she would go back to Naples and set up a small business in a dress shop or something similar, and that if our lot won she would do the same thing in England and lead a respectable life like any good Roman Catholic lady should.

We were told we would be moving on shortly so our problem was what to do with Jan Rossetti; we knew if we handed him in he would be a prisoner of war and something much worse would most likely happen to him for as he was dressed in civilian clothes he would be treated as a spy.

I asked him if he had any relations in Tripoli and he told us that he had an aunt on his mother's side of the family and that her name was Carla Anconi. He had never met her and didn't know where she lived. It was not a lot to go on in a place the size of Tripoli but we made our minds up that we would try to find her and ask if she would take him in.

When on coast patrol there was no need to have a wagon and driver so I had to think of a way to get Jan to his aunt in Tripoli.

Archie's tooth was the solution; he had been plagued with toothache for quite a while so now was the time to have it pulled out. I went with him to headquarters, saw the medical orderly and asked if I could have transport to take Archie to Tripoli to have his tooth pulled, hoping all the time that it would be a driver who had a soft heart and could keep his mouth shut.

There was no need to worry for who should turn up next morning but our ex-driver Frank and a fifteen hundredweight truck.

He was all for it so Yoddy, Jan and I piled in and off we went to the military hospital in Tripoli. We were hoping there would be a long queue at the dentists as we may be away a long time finding aunty, and knowing Archie we were afraid that if he was left to his own devices he would either finish up as drunk as a hand cart or get thrown out of a brothel window which had happened to him once before. It was no wonder the higher ups in the Air Force thought he was officer material.

It was obvious to us the place to look was in the Italian quarter and Frank had the good idea that we should ask around in the food shops. There were not many around as food was a bit short at that time. It was at the third shop that we found out where she lived; it was only in the next street at number nineteen.

There was a mud brick wall with a door in it. I banged on the door but no one answered so I gave it a push and it opened. What was inside came as a surprise after the grotty door; a courtyard with a lovely flower garden in the middle of it.

The house was at the far end of the courtyard, a table and chair were outside the door and that made me think that only one person lived there.

The house door was open and in the half light coming through the doorway towards us was a plump middle aged lady who looked frightened. Jan explained to her in Italian who he was, she threw her arms around him and tears of joy ran down her cheeks. I could see we would not have any problems regarding her looking after him.

She asked us to stay and have something to eat but we had Archie to pick up at the dentists and besides that I knew if she did give us any food it would mean her going without herself so we settled for a cup of ersatz coffee.

While we were drinking our coffee aunty and Jan were having what looked like a serious conversation. When Jan translated it to me I gathered that his aunt had a friend who worked on the docks and that she would have a word with him about getting him some casual work unloading the ships.

She also had a man friend who worked in the local government office who would most likely be able to fix him up with an identity card.

It amazed me how when people are living in adverse times that by hook or by crook they can get organised so quickly.

Archie had had his tooth out and we were on our way back to Zavia feeling smug about having done a good day's work and that everything had gone according to plan.

Our troops had already landed in Sicily so we could put our minds to rest about going on the invasion.

Some days later we got a message to report back to headquarters; it looked as if we were on the move again.

It was to Tripoli, past the columns of Romulus and Remus and on to the docks where we embarked a ship called the *Princess Kathleen* which took us to Malta. Some of the Liverpool lads knew it well for pre-war it had been a ferry on the Ireland or Isle of Man run.

Even though the ship anchored a half mile or so off Valletta's Grand Harbour it was easy to see the vast amount of damage that had been done by the continual bombing they had had.

After tiffin the next day a few of us went ashore in one of the ship's lifeboats. I don't know why we bothered for when we landed on the fish quay all I could see was a steep hill going up into the town and a street with a narrow path up the middle with piles of stones and rubble on each side. Behind the piles was what was left of the buildings.

When we were half way up the street the air raid sirens went off. Civilians appeared from nowhere and were running through an opening in the remains of a building at the side of the street so we followed them.

It was a cellar and by the look of it people had been living down there for a long time. A Cypriot man told me that the air raids had eased off and this was the first one that month.

At four o'clock we had to be back on the fish quay and that was all I saw of Valletta.

The next morning about ten o'clock I could tell by the activity of the crew we would soon be on the move.

I was leaning on the rail on the landward side of the ship having a last look at Valletta and wondering how the people had coped with the constant bombing of the last two or three years without going stark raving mad, when Harry Clark came up behind me and said, 'Come and have a look at this lot.' I followed him to the other side of the ship and saw a sight I will never forget.

There were warships sailing slowly towards us. To me they

looked like battleships, cruisers and destroyers etc. 'And that is only a part of our Mediterranean fleet,' said Harry.

He was wrong, for about two hours later an announcement came over the loudspeaker telling us that Italy had capitulated and the bulk of the Italian fleet had sailed into Valletta; a big cheer went up.

Things were getting better all the time.

It took us four or five days to reach Port Said and we only got attacked by enemy aircraft twice with no damage.

What protected the ships more than anything was that they flew a barrage balloon which made it difficult for enemy aircraft to dive over the full length of the ship without running into the wire from the balloon.

It was on the *Princess Kathleen* that I had my first nightmare. As usual when on board a ship I slept on the deck with my head to the side of the ship and my life jacket as a pillow. Harry was on one side of me and Smithie at the other.

I was in the corner furthest away from the bottom of the stairs in the cellar of the farmhouse in Tunisia, there was light coming through the wire grille high up in the wall and it was shining directly onto the mutilated bodies of the woman and the two children.

At the foot of the stairs was Ginger Mason pointing a rifle straight at me. By the look on his face I could tell he intended to use it. The first thing that came to my mind was that he had found out what I had done and taken it upon himself to be my executioner. I had my rifle with me so I brought it up to fire from the hip and slipped the safety catch off. All the time I was shouting and screaming, 'Don't Ginger, don't!'

I put pressure on my trigger but my finger was paralysed; I wondered if he was having the same problem as he didn't fire.

Eventually I woke up still shouting and screaming and jumping about.

I could hear Smithie saying, 'He's having a fit.'

Harry was at the other side stroking my head and saying, 'Calm down Gun, it's alright.'

The sweat was running off me and I didn't get to sleep again that night.

It was the first of many such nights.

After disembarking at Port Said we had to wait a few hours for the wagons to arrive as they had come down to Egypt by the coast road.

Why we hadn't travelled down on the wagons I don't know, maybe they thought the sea air would put a bit of colour in our cheeks.

We went to Cairo and as it was late in the day we camped that night near the fork in the road where one road goes back to Port Said, one goes up the desert and the other one goes down to Cairo. It seemed a long time since we were here before.

It was back to Helwan and meeting up once again with Warrant Officer Crocker the station WO. He was a strange chap for an SWO.

When he got a new lot of lads on parade for the first time his introduction went something like this. 'Now lads, I am Warrant Officer Crocker and I will never shout at you because it isn't nice to shout.' This was very unusual for an SWO. 'When I ask you to do something you can please yourselves whether you do it or not.' And then in a menacing tone of voice he would growl, 'But if you don't do what I ask you it will be God help you.'

When I got to know him he was a nice enough chap but meant every word he said.

After about a week at Helwan the CO informed us that we all had to learn to drive and we would be issued with jeeps in place of the wagons as we were going on an operation where there would be only four men to a post; two observers and two wireless opps who would have pack sets instead of the 1082-83s.

Harry Birkenhead taught me how to drive and I passed my test one Sunday morning in Cairo.

We had to find a way of getting enough gear on to the jeep to last us an indefinite length of time, what with that and the four of us it took some doing.

There is a small island in the Dodecanese group called Kos that is now a thriving holiday resort and that is where we went. By all accounts our troops had taken the island and the RAF had got the airfield going. What they didn't tell us was that the Germans had retaken it.

We landed from a landing craft onto a beach and were trying to get organised when all hell broke loose. There were Stukas dive-bombing us and shells dropping all over the place.

Every time we tried to get our aerial mast up a Hooray Henry army officer nearby shouted, 'Get that bloody aerial down. You are drawing their fire.'

Our headquarters was on a ship anchored a few miles off; we didn't manage to get in touch with them.

It wasn't long before the officer and his merry men started moving back down the beach and on to the boats we had landed from.

Later I heard that not long after our fiasco the British took Kos back again.

On arriving back at Helwan there was talk of the unit breaking up as radar was taking over. What we did visually radar could do from a distance.

We did one last operation before the unit broke up.

Winston Churchill, Roosevelt and Chiang Kai-shek were having a meeting at Mena House just outside Cairo and as a precaution our unit was putting a screen around Cairo.

Our post was plonked on top of the Great Pyramid at Giza. The top of the pyramid is a flat area about twenty feet square with a steel pole in the middle going up to what was its original height which we found handy for our aerial.

Some Egyptians carried most of the equipment up which was not easy. It was a struggle for us to climb up without carrying anything.

We were up there for four days; sometimes we could see the three great men in a garden behind the house.

One day a photographer from one of the English newspapers came and took a few snaps. Three months later Smithie received a letter from his mother with a photograph in it from the *News of the World* and there he was looking out through binoculars from the top of one of the wonders of the world.

After going back to Helwan we did a couple of weeks near a town called Fayum. Why we went there I never knew, unless it was to keep the mosquitoes busy. There was a lake near where we set up our post and it must have been the biggest breeding ground in Egypt for them.

Usually when you get bitten by a mosquito you get a little irritating lump but not so with these as all our forearms and legs were swollen up like balloons.

As soon as we got back to Helwan, our CO had us on parade and told us the bad news. It didn't come as a shock as we had been expecting it for a while. The 34 Wireless Observer Unit was to be disbanded. Some of the WOPs were going on a radar course at Heliopolis.

I was posted along with another corporal and fourteen other ranks to a new unit that had just arrived from England.

It was 39 WOU and was camped at kilometre 42 up the road to Alexandria.

The sight that met us when we arrived was unbelievable. The tents were all in lines with whitewashed stones marking out the paths. Where there were no paths the sand had been raked and there wasn't a footprint on it. At the front of the living tents there was a big tent with a square of whitewashed stones in front of it. In the middle of the square was a flagpole with the RAF flag fluttering in the breeze.

We got our kitbags off the wagon and dumped them in a heap by the flagpole. After we had stood there for twenty minutes a pale-faced weedy looking flying officer came out of the big tent.

He looked straight at me and shouted in a squeaky voice, 'Get these men into line and bring them to attention corporal.'

The last time I had given words of command was in 1940 at Watnall when I was promoted to LAC and had to have a go at giving orders to see who was fit to be promoted to Cpl. I wasn't promoted and it was a long time ago so all I could do was try my best.

It didn't work out too bad as I think the lads tried hard for my benefit. The flying officer seemed impressed.

He then gave us a lecture on what was expected of us and what our duties would be. I originally thought he was going to read the riot act to us.

One of the duties besides emptying the latrines, helping in the cookhouse and keeping the camp tidy was to give my lads half an hour each of foot and rifle drill every morning. The lads helped me with it and knew that my shouting and bawling at them was for the benefit of the jumped up CO.

It could have been worse. The men who had come out from Blighty with him had to do a ten mile route march across the desert every day. Maybe he realised we were old sweats and took it easy with us.

All of a sudden the toy soldier as we called him just disappeared with his kit in a fifteen hundredweight truck down the road to Cairo. Maybe he had been given a desk job as there were hundreds of desks in Cairo with officers like him propping them up.

After a day or two with the Flight Sgt. in charge, our new CO turned up. He was an army major from the Royal Artillery complete with swagger stick and breeches.

The morning after he arrived he had us all on parade and told us he wasn't a bull-shitter and to carry on as we had been doing but without the route marches. If we had any problems we were to take them to him and he would do his best to sort them out.

In between sentences he would give a large belch so he was immediately christened the Belching Major.

It seemed strange to have an army man in charge of an Air Force unit. His name was Major Alderson and we couldn't have done better. He was a gentleman who liked a drink or two. After he had been with us a few days he organised a day out in Cairo for us so we divided ourselves into groups of thirty and drew lots for who went first and so on.

I was in the third group so when it was our turn we went to the ancient capital of the Middle East in a three ton wagon which dropped us by the park in Sharia Soliman Pasha where the drivers said they would pick us up at 10pm.

I teamed up with two of the lads from our old unit, Shorty Frost, my old pal Archie and Cpl. Hunter, a lad who was in the new unit. He came from Northern Ireland so he was known as Paddy although his proper name was George. He had a great sense of humour so we soon became good mates.

The first thing we did was to go for a bottle of beer or two. There were two breweries in Cairo, the Lion and Stella that both did a decent brew.

After a snack at a WVS canteen and another drink or two we sauntered along looking at stalls and in shop windows.

They all displayed the same old junk that servicemen sent home to their mothers and girlfriends, half of which never reached its destination.

When looking in one shop window a cultured voice behind us said, 'If you boys are looking for presents to send home it is best not to buy them here in the main street because you will find the same things much cheaper in the back streets.' At first I thought he was a tout for some shop or other but I was wrong. He introduced himself and told us he was the first officer on a ship that had docked at Alexandria and that four weeks ago he had been in Glasgow.

Archie cottoned on straight away and was asking him about the bombing and how the people were coping etc.

For an Egyptian, he knew Glasgow like the back of his hand; not did he only know about Glasgow, he could talk about Belfast and London in a similar way. He invited us to go and have coffee with him and off we went.

His conversation was mostly about England so we were all ears.

After a while, when he thought he had gained our confidence, he told us the real reason for his trip to Cairo.

When his ship docked at Alexandria or Port Said he always paid a visit to a house in a suburb not far from here where some girl students lived and he had tea with them, a few drinks and an hour or two in bed with one of the girls.

What a life, it made our minds boggle. Shorty was the first one to say what we were all thinking.

His answer was that he had once taken some Australian soldiers and the girls looked on these little parties as a way to make a small sum of money to help towards their education. They did expect a little money in return for their favours but the Aussies had had their pleasure and run off without giving their donation. It left me hoping that the girls' education didn't suffer too much.

He thought we looked like decent lads and we could go with him to the house and see what he could do. If we gave him a pound each so he could go and pay the girls first, maybe they would be willing.

After clubbing together what money we had between us we found we were a pound short.

He studied a bit and suggested he could pay the other pound and he would give us the name of his ship so we could send it on to him if we were so inclined. He said he would like to keep in touch with us as he looked on us as friends.

It was about a mile to a nice area of the city with a tree lined street of well-kept houses with gardens at the front.

I never imagined there were such nice places so near the hustle and bustle of the city centre.

He asked us to wait at the end of the street while he went to the house to see if it was all right with the girls for us to pay them a visit.

We watched him go down the street and noted which house he went to so that if everything went according to plan we could pay it a visit on our own whenever we were in Cairo again.

He went to the fourth house down and went straight in through the front door.

After we waited twenty minutes or so he didn't appear and we began to get worried.

After half an hour it was panic stations and off we went to the fourth house down the street. Leaving my pals at the gate I went up to the door. It was open and before I knocked I noticed that there was a long hallway which led to another open door at the far end that looked like it went into a yard or back street. It didn't take me long to realise what had happened. He had gone straight through the house and out the back door.

I was standing there going red in the face with anger when a middle aged couple came down the passage, took one look at me and then at my pals at the gate and started shouting, 'Imshi yalla' over and over again, which in Arabic means 'go away quickly.'

The man had a big stick in his right hand so I went away quickly.

All I heard from the group going back into Cairo was four letter words and that our conman 'friend' was born out of wedlock.

Eventually we finished up sat on a wall outside the park in Sharia Soliman Pasha without an acker (slang for small Egyptian coin) between us.

This was a bit ironic as I would have had plenty of credits in my pay book with me not drawing any money when I was in the desert. Thankfully I had only drawn enough pay for my day out and the conman had taken that.

We sat there contemplating what to do with the four hours we had to spend before the wagon came when a Cpl. Marks came along and wanted to know what we were doing sat there looking as if the end of the world was at hand. I told him and amazingly he didn't laugh.

Cpl. Marks had been a wireless opp. on the old unit and now he was at Heliopolis on the radar course.

He was a loner and didn't seem to have any pals; maybe it was because he didn't drink or smoke. His family had a cigarette factory somewhere in Ireland and every now and again he would get a parcel of cigs from home so he dished them out among the lads.

He sat with us for a while and said he was going to the cinema and if we wanted to go with him he would pay.

On the way to the cinema he took us into a canteen and bought us chicken and chips even though he knew we may never see him again to repay him.

The film we went to see was Nelson Eddy and Jeanette MacDonald in Bitter Sweet, a sad film that didn't do much to cheer us up after the day we had had but it was better than sitting on the wall for hours feeling sorry for ourselves.

After saying thanks and farewell to Cpl. Marks it was time to make our way back to the wagon. It wasn't there and when we did find it the driver was sprawled out in the back in a drunken stupor and his cargo were all staggering about as drunk as handcarts.

Through no fault of our own there was only our little party that was sober so it was up to one of us to drive the wagon back to kilo 42. With me being the only NCO that wasn't drunk and having recently passed my driving test I dropped in for the job.

The wagon was a Dodge three tonner and I had learned to drive a Ford with a little experience on a Jeep.

Off we went and straight away I found that I couldn't get it from second gear into third. Whether I doubled the clutch or tried to take it straight through, it wouldn't have it.

Getting out of Cairo was a fiasco and going up the Alexandria Road wasn't much better. I don't think the drunks in the back knew anything about it and there wasn't a word said about it next morning and so it all blew over.

That night I had a bad nightmare; it was the same as before with the woman and the two children and Ginger at the bottom of the steps pointing his rifle at me. I must have carried on a bit because one or two of the lads who were not drunk complained about the row I had been making during the night.

I had come to the conclusion that if I had a drop or two of alcohol before going to sleep I could sleep the night through without any problems.

A 'drop or two' was five or six pints or the equivalent in spirits. The trouble was that we were not always in a position where I could obtain my medication, so to speak.

12
Beirut and Jerusalem

Another two days at kilo 42 and then we got the order to move.

The day before we set off I received a nice bunch of letters from Jean and two from home, so after I had packed my gear I spent an hour or two writing letters, which was a difficult job as we hadn't to say where we were, where we were going or what we were doing.

My letters to Jean were all about how much I missed her, how much I loved her and our plans for when it was all over.

Our journey on the first day took us through Cairo and along the road towards the Suez Canal. The traffic through Cairo was so bad that we only got to the other side of Heliopolis before making our first stop for the night.

The next day we got to the canal early but there was a long queue of service vehicles at the ferry, so we were held up there for a few hours giving us plenty of time to gorge ourselves on half a tin of bully beef and a packet of biscuits.

It was no wonder there was a long queue, it was the same ferry we had used before and it only carried two wagons. The only difference was that there were now two Arabs to wind the handle instead of one. When we got to the other side of the canal the ferrymen had a smoke while we got the wagons off.

On this side of the canal was the Sinai desert where we camped for the night, on the other side was the town of Ismalia. That night three of my mates and I went across to Ismalia for a night out. There was only one man working the ferry so we had to take it in turns winding the other handle.

When we had worked our passage and got to the other side he had the cheek to ask for baksheesh. We were in good spirits at the thoughts of a night on the town so we clubbed together and gave him a few ackers.

He then told us the ferry finished at ten o'clock and that he would leave moored to the bank a jolly boat we could use if it was after ten when we got back to the ferry. If we hadn't given him the ackers I don't think that he would have told us about the boat.

There were a few bars in Ismalia catering for the thousands of troops that were stationed in the canal area at the time. Besides drink they all had a set menu which was chicken and chips or, for something different, chips and chicken.

After strolling around the town for a while we found a bar that we liked the look of and got settled in.

Seeing that there were four of us, a round was a bottle of vodka and chicken and chips four times. This meant that by the end of the night we had all had a bottle of vodka each and four helpings of chicken and chips.

During the evening an Arab snake charmer came into the bar fully equipped with his snake, basket and flute. After his performance, which he must have done in every bar in the town every night (it was no wonder his snake looked tired), he came round asking for baksheesh.

When he returned to his basket he put his head in his hands and started moaning and sobbing. His snake had gone. Everyone was on the floor crawling about looking for it. The bar owner was going frantic and shouting that he would not let him in his bar again with or without his snake and off he went still crying about the loss of his livelihood.

After leaving the bar we all went staggering along the street. At the end was the poor old snake charmer, sat cross legged on the ground still crying and still with his basket and flute. We all felt sorry for him and Archie suggested that we had a whip round to buy him a new snake. At this, Shorty put his hand down his shirt and pulled out the snake. He had taken it when its owner was going round collecting his baksheesh. Seeing this, the charmer stopped crying and started voicing a few Arabic swearwords that involved Shorty, his sisters, his mother, his father and a few uncles.

Reaching the canal at well after the ferryman's knocking off time we found the boat was indeed moored, but on the other side of the canal.

At first we thought that someone would eventually come across to our side so all we had to do was wait, which is something that you become expert at in the forces.

After waiting a long time Smithie, the clever one of our quartet said, 'Who would be coming from the desert side of the canal at this time of night?' He was right, who would?

In the end it came to a toss of a coin to see who the lucky boy was who would swim across and bring the boat back. Guess what? It was me.

One of the kinder types in the party offered to look after my boots and cap and in I went. Although it was winter, the water did not feel as cold as I thought it would but it was still cold enough to sober me up a bit.

My favourite stroke for going a long way in a long time was sidestroke, otherwise known as the lazy stroke, so off I went heading straight across.

Every now and again I stopped to have a rest and look to see how much further I had to go; I was beginning to panic a bit as the other side did not seem to be getting much closer.

About half an hour passed before I did reach the other side, knackered, wet through and no boots and all I could see before me disappearing into the gloom was stony ground.

After doing a bit of advanced maths I worked out that I must have been swept about a mile down the canal. No one had told me at school there was a strong current from Port Said to the Suez end.

I set off walking in the opposite direction to the way I had drifted and it was not so pleasant in the dark without my boots on. Fortunately the soles of my feet had got a bit hard as I had not worn anything on my feet whenever we were in the deserts.

At last I came to a tented camp and as I wandered on through the lines of tents I could hear men snoring and talking in their sleep, the language sounded like Hindu.

At the camp entrance there were two Indian soldiers complete with turbans and beards, half asleep, leaning on their rifles.

I coughed to let them know I was there hoping that I wouldn't surprise them enough to spring into action as they had their bayonets fixed.

Once aware of my presence they just stood there staring at me as if they had seen a ghost. I expect it did look strange; me standing there wet through and nothing on my feet.

When they had got over the shock one of them said in a broad Lancashire accent, 'What happened to you?'

It turned out that he had been brought up in Rochdale and when he joined up he had enlisted in the Indian army.

They directed me to the road where the unit was camped, which wasn't far away, and so ended my night out in Ismalia.

When I got to the wagon my three comrades, if you can call them that, were all curled up fast asleep in their bedrolls at the side of the wagon. I did think of waking them and asking them if they wanted to piss but instead I got my bedroll out of the wagon and got my head down.

Next morning they looked a bit sheepish and told me that they had watched me making good progress across the canal even though the current was sweeping me down towards the Bitter Lakes. It seemed that not long after I had set off, two army lads arrived at the other side and brought the boat across.

It was cold next morning so I sat with my blanket round me eating my porridge, a hard-boiled egg, a packet of biscuits and a nice pot of tea. What made me feel colder was that my clothes were still wet from the night before.

When we were all together as a unit the cooking arrangements were much better because the unit cook and his mate cooked for all of us.

Crossing the Sinai desert was much the same as last time, except this time we were going the other way and after two days we got to Bea-Sheba and travelled on to Gaza in Palestine.

On our arrival at Gaza, Major Alderson had us all on parade and told us that we would be having a full day's rest and there were plenty of bars in the town as well as other things that catered for the likes of us.

I hoped they catered for the likes of him in the officers-only establishments as we were finding out he was one of the best without being soft with us.

By half past ten we had had our first round of drinks and by one o'clock were singing bawdy songs and making a nuisance of ourselves, so much so that the owner asked us to leave.

On our way into town we had seen a tattoo shop and Shorty suggested we all had a tattoo, so we staggered back to the shop.

When we got there it was closed for prayer time and I was glad as my dad had always warned me that if you had a tattoo it was the easiest way of being identified by the police or anyone else who may be looking for you.

Opposite the tattoo shop was a Turkish baths and since none of us had ever indulged in that kind of thing before we decided to give it a go.

The actual bathroom was in the basement so we followed the attendant down the stairs into what looked like a torture chamber. This, of course, was after we had paid our entrance fee so there was no running away.

The whole of the room was tiled with water running down the walls and as the water hit the floor it came up in clouds of steam.

In the middle of the floor was a marble slab raised up three feet and against the wall was a marble bench to sit on until the steam got working on us.

While we were sat there with the sweat oozing out of us the Arab attendant told us how it worked and some history about the place.

Underneath the tiled floors were fires that heated the water to make the steam. The floor being so hot meant we had to wear wooden sandals. He also told us that the baths had been built by the Romans when Palestine was part of the Roman Empire. On looking around the place I could well believe him.

After we had cooked a while he asked who was to be first on the slab. Smithie, showing off as usual, volunteered.

The big Arab got him face down and began pummelling his back as if he was trying to break every bone in his body. He then donned his rubber pads and got cracking. I could actually see two years of dirt and grime coming to the surface. I would like to bet that by the time he had finished the four of us his Turkish bath would need a good swill out.

It turned out a bit expensive but it sobered us up and kept us away from the tattoo parlour.

Early next morning we were on our way again, sticking more or less to the coast road north to Nathanya, Haifa, Tyre, Sidon etc. camping at night outside each town and by doing so managing to get a drop to drink.

My problem now was that if I drank a sufficient amount of alcohol before I got my head down for the night I didn't have the nightmare but on nights when I didn't have a drop or two to drink it was an even money bet I would be back in the cellar in Tunisia with the mother and children and Ginger Mason threatening to shoot me.

At last we were in the Lebanon and heading for the then lovely city of Beirut.

We parked on some spare land by the airport and Major Alderson went into the city, presumably to find out where we would be staying. He came back with a big smile on his beery face and off we went towards the city that could be seen in the distance.

On the coast, in a sparsely built-up area on the outskirts, we turned off down a steep street that went to the beach. A little way along the street, on the right hand side, was a big double gate with a sentry box on either side.

Through the gates was a barrack square and an imposing looking three storey building which was the barracks. It had been a French Foreign Legion barracks when the Lebanon was a thriving French colony.

The French didn't thrive there any more as the Arab community had come to the conclusion they had more right to the place than the French.

On the ground floor of the building were the cookhouse, the NAAFI canteen and the stores. On the first and second floors was a balcony going the full length of the building with five barrack rooms leading off from each balcony. The first floor was occupied by an army signals unit.

The top floor was identical to the second and it was to be our home for the next few months. Our address was Saint Elle Barracks, Middle East Forces.

It seemed strange being in a building after sleeping rough for over two years. We still slept on the floor but having a roof over our heads was a luxury.

The next morning Major Alderson had us on parade and told us more or less what we would be doing while we were at Beirut and that he had no idea how long our stay would be.

He must have been up half the night working out a syllabus for us and it went something like this. The Observers and WOPs would be split up into three squads with two corporals to each squad. From nine until ten each morning except Saturday and Sunday the corporals would give the squads an hours foot and rifle drill. At ten o'clock there would be a break for a brew until ten-thirty.

After that there were to be lessons bringing us up to scratch with aircraft recognition, small arms, map reading and anything else that we needed to brush up on. The drivers would be doing maintenance on the vehicles and transport duties when required. In the afternoons we would do exercises in the hills and route marches with Wednesday afternoons for recreation. Saturday mornings were for make do and mend and doing our washing, with Saturday afternoon and Sunday at leisure.

Although the major seemed an easy going type he had things pretty well worked out. I have noticed since through my life that people who make their work look easy are usually good at their job.

Corporal (Paddy) Hunter and I picked out thirty lads that we knew and we were in business.

All was going well; there was a bar just along the coast road towards Beirut owned by a man called Yosef Adid with whom I became a good friend and customer.

I didn't visit the bar every night as he sold bottles to take out, I had got well and truly hooked on vodka and I found that if I had enough of it before getting my head down I would sleep through without having the nightmares.

There was another Cpl. in the room called Bill Bailey and he was also giving the vodka some stick so on some nights we would stay in and have a little session in the barrack room. When we had had a drink or two we would sing 'Won't you come home Bill Bailey?' and lots of other songs of a more bawdy nature, and all the other lads would join in.

We were having a good time at Saint Elle barracks until one night there was a really bad storm. The wind was blowing at gale force off the sea and the rain was coming down in torrents when one of the lads said that he could hear a plane. I thought that he was imagining things but just after there was a dull crunching noise from somewhere up in the hills and we all went quiet.

On parade next morning Major Alderson joined us. I knew that it must be something serious as he didn't usually show his face before ten o'clock and on this occasion his face looked none too happy.

The first thing that came to mind was 'are we on the move again?' I was, but not too far away.

He informed us that a plane had crashed up in the hills in a village called Ali.

At that moment a fifteen hundredweight van came through the gates and on to the square. Out stepped a wing commander who conversed with the major for about five minutes and he then went on to explain the situation to us which was that all five members of the crew were dead.

The plane had crashed into the basement of a house on the mountain and the house had come down on top of the aircraft burying most of it in stones and rubble.

Major Anderson then took over saying that the RAF had asked for our assistance in uncovering the aircraft and getting the bodies out.

He then looked straight at me and said, 'Corporal Davidson, I know you have done this kind of thing before so I would like you to take another corporal and eight men and see what you can do.'

Paddy, my Irish mate, asked if he could go as he had never done this kind of thing before, so it was him, Archie, Smithy and six other lads from the old unit.

We went to the stores on the ground floor and drew picks and shovels, hacksaws, a cooking stove, two tents and rations. The major was there to supervise and see that we got plenty of rations. The wing commander had ordered five coffins from a joiner's shop in Beirut that would be brought up to the site when they were ready.

All we had to do now was pack our small kits and be on our way up the mountain to the village of Ali.

When we got there and saw the crash it looked a bit daunting to say the least.

The front of the house was two storeys high and on the road side but with it being built on a slope the back of the house was three storeys high, and the plane, a Boston, had gone straight into the basement.

After scratching my head, looking at the mess and trying to figure out the best way of tackling the job we brewed up and had something to eat.

I then had a look round and found a nice flat grassy patch on which to pitch our tents and make ourselves comfortable for it looked as if we were going to be there for a good few days. I decided that it would be best to spend the remainder of the day having a rest and getting to know the village.

Some of the lads were knackered already so Paddy and I and a couple of the more adventurous types went for a look round and left the others to look after the rifles and equipment as there was some of the Ali lads hanging about casting their beady eyes over everything.

The village of Ali wasn't what you could call a metropolis; it had a Greek Orthodox Church and a general store that seemed to sell everything, including alcohol. Most of their booze stock was Retsina but they also had Arak which is a very potent drink that when mixed with water turns white. So I bought a bottle for my nightcap.

Our plan of attack was to first get the stones and rubble off what was left of the front part of the aircraft.

I have found through my life whenever I set out to do a job of work that there is some tool or other I have either forgotten or not thought of and, in this case, it was a couple of wheelbarrows. Luckily for us, Major Alderson turned up in the middle of the morning to see if we had got settled in. I told him about the barrows and his driver came up with them in the afternoon.

Not long after we had started work an Arab came along. He was waving his arms about, shouting non-stop in Arabic and jumping up and down. Eventually I realised it was his house. He didn't appreciate how lucky he was to have been sleeping at another house up the road that night. He kept going on about barley and oil he had stored in the basement and for us to be careful not to damage the containers when we got to them.

It was on the third day when we did get to them and although they were stored in large earthenware jars most of them were still intact. We also found the body of a woman who happened to be his wife but in his excitement he hadn't bothered to tell us about her.

Not long after finding the body a dozen or so of her relations came. They were all screaming and making that strange warbling sound that Arab ladies make at funerals. They then wrapped her in a white cloth and took her away. While all this was going on her husband was still wittering on about the broken jars.

After a while Paddy lost his temper, kicked his arse and told him to 'Imshi yalla!' which he did.

It was now a matter of turning our attention to the aircraft. The forward section was in bits so we gathered them as best we could and stacked them up. We then manhandled the engines out and up against a wall.

As we got into what was left of the fuselage we started finding bits of human remains; the biggest piece we found was the top end of a torso with no head and half an arm.

When the coffins arrived all we could do was wrap a few bits and pieces in a blanket and put an identity disk with them into each coffin.

The airmen were all South Africans. Before the plane had crashed one of the crew had been writing a letter home on an airmail letter pad and death had come so suddenly that the writing had stopped in the middle of a word.

The guns and ammunition were more or less intact, which surprised me as I thought the ammunition would have ignited on impact. We took the armaments to the tents for safe keeping.

During the fifth night Paddy woke me up telling me not to make a noise and listen. I could hear a grating noise coming from the direction of the aircraft.

We grabbed our rifles and went quietly to where the sound was coming from.

I couldn't believe my eyes at what I saw, there were two Arabs sawing away at the tailplane with large hacksaws. They had a donkey and cart standing by with a good load of aluminium already on it.

At first they just stood there dumbfounded and then both started speaking at the same time telling us how poor they were and that they had no food for their children, and if we reported them to the police they would be beaten and put in prison.

I got my thinking cap on and it didn't take long to work out something that would be beneficial to the two villains and us.

After a good deal of haggling the transaction came to a sum of two hundred Lebanese pounds which equalled about two pounds Sterling each shared with the other lads. This was just about enough for a good night out in Beirut but it wasn't much if we had been found out.

One more night and they had shifted the lot which was just as well because the next afternoon an air force sergeant and two airmen came with a Queen Mary (a sixty foot articulated vehicle used for transporting aircraft) to move the wreckage.

What was needed here was another bit of quick thinking and the best I could do on the spur of the moment was to tell them that some lads had been from Damascus two days before and said that they would be coming back for the engines and guns etc. in a few days' time.

The sergeant was annoyed, as they had come all the way from St. Jean in Palestine, and he said it was the second time in a month it had happened to them. So he decided to take what was left and let them from Damascus get stuffed.

We made them a brew, a good doffing of stew and had a chat. Then they were much happier and went on their way to St. Jean and we never heard another thing about it.

On getting back to the barracks at Beirut I soon got into the old routine of drill in the mornings, followed by map reading etc. and the afternoons free unless we had an exercise or route march. It was the life of Riley.

At Yosef Adid's bar on the coast road I had got friendly with an Arab taxi driver and sold him two Beretta pistols I had picked up in North Africa. I got eight pounds Sterling each for them. It wasn't really worth the risk as at the time the military police had units all over the Middle East called the Special Investigation Bureau (SIB) who went around dressed as civilians trying to talk service men into doing dodgy deals and then running them in.

One morning Major Alderson came on first parade and told us that the following day we were going on a map reading and survival exercise for two days. We had to go in pairs, so the next morning Paddy and I set off up into the mountains with a compass, ordnance map, rifles and back packs. The weather was fine and after we had climbed the thousand feet or so the going became easy and there was plenty of scrub around to make a fire so we had a brew with our bully beef and biscuits.

Before it got dark we started looking for a place to bivvy for the night when Paddy saw what looked like a monastery on a hillside about a mile away. If we were in luck there was a chance the monks would give us shelter for the night so we went to investigate.

There was a high wall round the grounds and after walking next to it for a short distance we came to a big wooden door with a metal ring attached to a rope that passed through a hole in the wood. Giving it a good pull started a bell clanging somewhere on the other side. Until then I hadn't noticed how quiet our surroundings were. There was no reply so I gave the rope another tug, thinking if there was no reply this time we would go back to our original plan of sleeping rough.

Just as we turned to go away the door was opened by what looked like a Greek Orthodox monk. I found out later that they belonged to a French order.

He took us into a big room in the main building, went away and came back with another monk who I took to be the head lad. He asked us what we wanted in perfect English, so I thought up a cock and bull story quickly and told him we had lost our way and didn't like the idea of trying to find our way back to Beirut in the dark.

On entering the room I had noticed a holy water font by the side of the door so, being a good Roman Catholic and a prize con-man, I had dipped my fingers in the font and made the sign of the Cross. It may have been this that found us shelter for the night. I always knew my Catholic education would come in handy some day.

He sat us on a form at a long table and after a while another monk brought us some water and a big piece of barley bread.

After our refreshment the head monk came back and took us to our cell. This was furnished with two straw palliasses and a crucifix on the wall. It was all a bit austere but no worse than what we were accustomed to and, anyway, beggars can't be choosers.

The next morning I was awakened by the chanting of the monks in another part of the building. After a while we made our way to the big room and thanked the head monk for our night's lodgings. He insisted we should have something to eat so we put our backpacks and rifles in a corner and joined in with their prayer which I gathered to be Grace before meals.

When the food came it was a piece of barley bread, a hard boiled egg and water. It was no wonder they all looked thin and hungry.

After the breakfast we went to say farewell to the boss and

found that you never get something for nothing. He asked if we would do a small task for him. He didn't wait for our reply, he just turned round and said, 'Follow me.' We eventually found ourselves at the bottom of the bell tower where there was a coil of new rope. I didn't need to be told what the task was, for up at the top of the tower was a bell with a tatty bit of rope hanging from it. Halfway up the tower was a platform with a crude-looking ladder leading up to it. On the platform was another ladder going up to a wooden beam with the bell dangling from it. We went up one at a time as the ladders didn't look too safe. Paddy tied the loose end round his waist and went up with me following.

Untying the old rope and tying on the new one was a tricky job but I realised that it would have been trickier still for the monks in their long frocks.

We parted company and went on our way with promises from the head monk that they would remember us in their prayers. It was a lovely morning and easy going back down to the barracks so, all in all, it had been a pleasant exercise and a novel experience to boot.

After a few days back at the barracks I was on the beach with a squad of lads instructing them in bayonet fighting, which I had learned a little bit about at Watnall in the early days.

After a while, when you have done the basics i.e. the vulnerable points, the high port, parrying and the butt stroke, it becomes a bit boring so I ordered the lads to double march to the end of the beach where there was an overhanging cliff which meant they couldn't be seen from the barracks. I told them to sit down and have a smoke and take it easy for the remainder of the lesson.

Looking back along the beach I saw one chap from the squad standing in the middle of the beach looking out to sea, most likely dreaming of his loved ones at home. His name was Smith and he came from Bradford, my home town. He was a bit of loner and I had had problems with him before.

I shouted for him to join us at the double. When he reached us I called him a stupid bastard and told him if the major had seen us from his balcony we would all be in the shit.

Little did I know then what trouble those few words were going to cause me in the future.

The next morning Major Alderson sent for me. Smith had

reported me for calling him a bastard and that is the one thing you have not to accuse anyone of in the forces.

I came out with a silly excuse, telling him that sometimes when I lost my temper I had mental lapses and I didn't know what I was saying half of the time.

At that he ordered me to go and see the medical officer in the morning and find out what he had to say about it.

I thought it was the major's way of punishing me, for if anyone went to see the MO it was all round the barracks in quick time that you had a dose of clap.

With the sixteen pounds I had got for the pistols and the credits that had mounted up in my pay book I decided to send some money home to my mother and buy a nice little watch to send to Jean (which never got there).

If you sent more money home than you were getting in your pay you had to fill in a form saying how you had come by it. I said I had won it at the races as there was a nice racecourse in Beirut where I sometimes went on a Saturday afternoon.

No sooner had I filled the form in when the major sent for me to go see him in his office. I panicked, wondering if he had found out about the pistols or the aluminium or both. I had no need to worry as all he wanted to know was which part of the racecourse I went in and could he meet me there next Saturday afternoon as he had been going for weeks and had hardly backed a winner. We arranged to meet and, following my expert advice, he didn't back a winner that day either. All I could say was, 'We all have our losing days, sir.' He didn't ask me to go with him again.

At night I was still having my medicinal vodka to keep off the nightmares and Jean's letters were getting to a stage where she was making plans for our future more than ever and it had me worried. It was not a matter of me not wanting to spend the future with her but would she be able to put up with the nightmares or the alcohol which prevented me having them? It had me worried, to say the least.

One morning, out of the blue, Major Alderson told us we were to have two weeks' leave. It came as a bit of a shock as up to now we had never thought about leave.

Previously, when we hit a town we just enjoyed ourselves as best we could and went on our way; it was something like you see in cowboy films.

After giving it some thought, Paddy suggested we hitch-hiked to Jerusalem. He wasn't a religious type but thought it would be interesting and I fully agreed so, after getting our passes and drawing some pay, we went.

The journey down the coast to Haifa, where we decided to stay the night, was plain sailing. Plenty of service vehicles were going south so we didn't have to wait long for lifts.

We reached Haifa in the evening and found a little bed and breakfast place and booked in for the night. We got something to eat and then found a bar where I could get my medicine to make sure I would have a good night's sleep.

Paddy wasn't a big drinker but like most of the Irish he had a great sense of humour and was good company which made for a jolly night out.

In the morning we had the usual boiled egg and jam and bread. It always seemed strange to me that in the Middle East there was an abundance of eggs but I rarely saw any hens.

By late afternoon we arrived in Jerusalem. It didn't take us long to find the YMCA hostel where we booked in for a week.

A young lady took us to a guest house where we were to have bed and breakfast and we would have our lunch and dinner at the YMCA canteen.

On the notice board at the hostel was a leaflet about members of the forces being invited to go on a five-day pilgrimage visiting places of interest with a guide. It was free, so without any hesitation we put our names down on the list provided.

Our guide was an Arab and he was brilliant. If he had been Christian or Jewish I have a feeling that we would have got a biased opinion but with him being a Muslim we got the straight-forward logical history.

I can't remember now the exact days of the places we visited. One day it was the Garden of Gethsemane and the Mount of Olives, another day it was Bethlehem, the Via Dolorosa and the Church of the Holy Sepulchre, the Dome of the Rock and so on. One morning he showed us the Potters' field that was bought with the thirty pieces of silver Judas received for betraying Christ. Another morning he plonked us on donkeys and led us through the gate into the old city where Christ was said to have gone through on Palm Sunday.

All in all I was glad Paddy had suggested the trip to Jerusalem.

I have been there since but I always look on that time as the best.

At the end of the week, after paying the money we owed at the hostel, we had no money left to see us all the way back to Beirut.

I asked the man at the desk if he knew of anywhere in Jerusalem where we could draw money on our pay books. He didn't know of anywhere.

There was a soldier standing behind me who had overheard my conversation and he asked where we were making for. I told him we were going to the coast and then up to Beirut. He called his pal over and he told us there was a leave camp on the coast at a place called Nathanya where we may be able to draw some money.

This was good news, for even if we couldn't draw any money we would still be able to get some grub and a night's kip.

It was late in the afternoon by the time we had found the camp.

At the reception there was a sergeant major; after explaining to him about our journey we wondered if it would be possible to draw some money. He told us we could but it would be in the morning and that we would be welcome to stay for our tea and breakfast before drawing some money from the pay accounts officer.

Still not having any money worried me as with no drink before going to bed I was sure I would have my nightmare. Luckily I didn't have one that night.

When he had shown us to our tents he asked what I thought at the time was a strange question. He asked us if we could ride. I said 'Horses?' and he said 'Mules.' I asked him why and he told us if we were willing to stay until tomorrow afternoon they were having mule races and there was a prize of thirty shillings (one pound fifty pence) for the winner of each race.

While I was deciding not to bother Paddy had already got fixed up for the two o'clock race. He was full of confidence and told me he had been brought up on a farm and was used to horses.

The next morning we drew some money and went to have a look at the racecourse. When I saw it I was glad I hadn't volunteered as there were hurdles about every hundred yards. They were not big but I wouldn't have liked the idea of charging over them on the back of a mule.

Paddy won his race easily, drew his winnings, thanked the sergeant major and off we went with money in our pockets for drink and a comfortable bed for the night.

It didn't take us long to find a nice little hotel as Nathanya was a popular Jewish holiday resort at that time.

On arriving back at Beirut we found out why we had been there in the first place. It seemed that Britain and the Yanks had been trying to talk Turkey into coming into the war on our side but they had thought it better to stay neutral.

This made things much better for us, for if Turkey had entered the war it would have meant us and a lot more lads going across the Dardanelles which in the First World War ended up as a massacre. Not that it mattered a great deal to the men at the top sitting in their London offices saying, 'We can afford to lose a hundred thousand here or a hundred thousand there.' What they never seem to think about is that all these men have families at home just the same as they have.

There was now talk of us going back to Egypt.

I had got to like Beirut. There was the American University with its football ground where they had lots of inter-services games. In the city near the docks were the bars and brothels for the other ranks, with names such as Susie's Joint, the Hole in the Roof, Folies Berger etc.

The brothels for officers were up a street in a better class area. The only difference between the other ranks and the officers' brothels was that if you got venereal disease (VD) in an officers' brothel it was known as parson's clap, which was said to be the kind of VD you get off toilet seats!

The out of bounds brothels were down some streets on the right hand side of the Place de Canons looking down towards the sea. To make sure we knew these places were out of bounds, at the top of each street there was a circular piece of metal suspended on two wires slung across the street. The discs were painted white with a red line around the edge and another red line going from top to bottom down the centre and they were known as the streets of the flaming arseholes.

For healthier minded innocents like myself there were nice beaches to go swimming from and pleasant walks along the coast.

But it wasn't long before we were packing our gear and under way once again to the land of the Pharaohs. Down the coast to Gaza, camping each night near some town or other where we could get some liquid refreshment to slake the dust from the day's journey; the major always tried to cater for our needs besides his own.

One night, when crossing the Sinai Desert, I ran out of vodka and had a bad nightmare.

On reaching Ismalia we headed south to a transit camp at a place called Kasfareet on the western side of the Great Bitter Lake which is a part of the Suez Canal. As it was a transit camp I knew we wouldn't be there for long.

On the first morning the camp warrant officer had us on parade to dole out fatigues, i.e. cleaning and emptying the latrines, cookhouse duties and whitewashing the stones that mark out the roads etc.

He picked me out straight away. 'Right, corporal do you know anything about gardening?'

If I had said yes he would most likely have told me there was a piano to move so I said, 'No, sir,' which didn't make any difference as I finished up with six men, a handcart with eight young palm trees on it and some picks and shovels.

On the side of the lake there was a canteen with a piece of level ground at its front and a few tables and chairs were placed on it.

The job was to plant the trees in a line about four feet from the water's edge making sure that we dug the holes deep enough for the roots to be able to reach the water.

Even though I didn't know anything about gardening we must have made a good job of it for about two years later I was on a train going from Ismalia down to Suez and saw the trees in all their glory and they looked in fine fettle. There was a sergeant with me called Charlie and when I told him that I had planted them he looked at me as if I had lost my marbles.

No one had informed us as yet where we were going. On the second morning they gave us three inoculations so everyone was sure we were heading for the Far East. The method used for receiving the inoculations was that we formed a circle with the leading man of the circle having a piece of cloth tied round his arm, and when he got to the table again the medical orderly knew it was time to change the serum. They only changed the needle when it became blunt.

The next morning we had to parade to get our money changed and lo and behold they gave us English money. Most of us got drunk in the canteen that night.

Next morning we were on a ship at Suez called the *Stratheden* bound for our green and pleasant land. We hadn't had the chance to write home to tell them we were coming.

It was a small convoy and we only got attacked twice somewhere between Malta and Gibraltar.

About three hundred yards from us on the starboard side was an ack-ack ship bristling with pom-pom guns, so enemy aircraft were wary about coming in too close.

It was a much more pleasant voyage than the one we went out on. There was much more room, although I still slept in my favourite spot on the deck with my head to the side of the ship and my life jacket for a pillow. The food was better and we were on our way home.

After we had passed Gibraltar and were off the coast of Portugal the weather was fine, the sea was calm and the little villages on the hillsides looked so peaceful I couldn't imagine there was a war on.

Everybody was estimating how many days it would be before we reached England, some of the clever ones were counting the hours.

Crossing the Bay of Biscay the sea was like a mill pond. After that it was the western approaches, which a couple of years ago would have been teeming with U-boats. Probably there were still plenty about, but resting on the sea bed with crews still in them; what a waste of young men war is.

As we were sailing up the Irish Sea there were lots of warships heading south. They seemed to have a sense of urgency about them. It was two days before I found out just how urgent they were.

We all thought that we would be putting in at Liverpool but we didn't.

When passing Anglesey and the approaches to the Mersey my mind drifted back to that grim February day when I was leaving Liverpool on the *Duchess of Richmond*. I thought about the soldier leaning on the ship's rail beside me with tears running down his cheeks saying, 'We may never see England again.' I wonder again if he did?

At last we were heading up the Clyde to Glasgow passing by Gourock, Greenock and Dunoon. How lovely and green the fields and trees looked after the deserts I had seen.

It amazed me how narrow the river was as we got nearer the docks and how high the ship was, for when I looked over the rail from the deck the roofs of the buildings were a long way below.

We docked in Princess Dock and no sooner had the ship tied up than an officer, a sergeant and a military policeman, came on to the mess deck and ordered us to come out to the deck space at the end of the tables three at a time and empty the contents of our kitbags on to the deck, so as to make sure we were not going to smuggle any contraband into our beloved country.

Luckily one of the crew had warned me about this; I didn't believe him at the time as I thought he was pulling my leg, but just in case I had unscrewed one of the grilles from a ventilator with my jack knife and hidden a few hundred cigs in the shaft.

In the afternoon I was, as usual, leaning on the rail with Archie and on the dock was a tram with its destination on the front, it was going to Maryhill. Archie looked at me, smiled and said, 'I live at 1937 Maryhill Road.' It was so near and yet so far. It strikes me as strange how that address has stuck in my memory all those years.

About nine or ten o'clock that night we disembarked. At the bottom of the gangplank was a bevy of military police shouting, 'Come on you lazy buggers, hurry up and get on the wagons.' There was no heroes' return in those days.

13
England

The wagons took us to the station where we boarded a train and arrived at Blackpool, of all places, at about four o'clock on the morning of the sixth of June 1944.

From the station a sergeant marched us to the football ground where we put our blankets and lots of other kit that had deteriorated a bit during our travels on to a fire in the car park.

From there he took us to a long space underneath the grandstand which looked as if it might have been a bar in happier times. There was a row of tables with tired looking WAAFs sat behind them. I went to a table with a big letter D for Davidson on it. The girl took my particulars from my pay book and gave me an address to go to in Crystal Road. Not knowing Blackpool I asked her where to go and she said, 'It's somewhere between the Tower and the Pleasure Beach.' What she didn't tell me was that nearly all Blackpool is between the Tower and the Pleasure Beach.

Next job was to draw some pay at a table at the top end of the shed and get a ration card for the landlady at the digs in Crystal Road.

Off I went with Paddy, Tommy Lawson, Archie and a Taffy called Buckley to try and find our five star hotel, humping what was left of our kit along with our rifles and bayonets.

I had often heard the phrase 'A face like a Blackpool boarding house keeper.' but I had never seen one until now. She greeted us with 'Wipe your feet and follow me,' which we did all the way up to the crows' nest, an attic with four army beds in it. She then asked us for our ration cards. We didn't know at the time that she had holiday makers in the rooms downstairs and she needed our ration cards to supplement their rations.

Before she left she told us the house rules. We hadn't to make a noise, we had to be in by 10pm and we were expected to help in the kitchen with the washing up. At this point in her rules I told her to get lost and she then threatened to report me to the warrant officer.

By now it was only 7am so Paddy and I decided to have a walk along the front and see if we could find somewhere to get breakfast.

We headed towards the Pleasure Beach and eventually came to a place that had been well known in peacetime as Pablo's ice cream parlour. It was now a forces' canteen but it didn't open until eight o'clock so we sat on the steps to wait.

At dead-on eight o'clock a lady came and opened the door to let us in.

There was a radio on the counter and the newsreader was just announcing that our troops had started landing on the beaches of Normandy earlier that morning. I couldn't believe what I was hearing as we had been under the impression it was the invasion they had been rushing us back to England for.

All Paddy said was, 'And the best of British luck to them.'

We then had our first breakfast in a long time of bacon, eggs, beans and fried bread.

We had to be back on parade at Crystal Road at nine o'clock with a lot of other lads that were billeted round about, for the sergeant to put us in the picture as to what we would be doing for the next day or so.

The first thing we had to do was go to Marks and Spencer's, now an RAF stores, and hand in our uniforms and be given new ones.

When I was in the mountains in northern Iran I had a confrontation with a wild boar and in my panic I had defended myself by hitting it on the head with my rifle and breaking it off at the small of the butt. I had fixed the butt back on with a couple of nails and bound it with string.

The corporal in the stores was a surly looking chap and when he saw the state of my rifle he went blue in the face and screeched, 'I can't take it like that!'

I tried to stay calm and said, 'Well I've finished with it.'

He calmed down a bit and asked, 'What can I do with a rifle in that state?'

So I told him what to do and thick end first.

It was the second time on my first day in England that I was to be reported to the warrant officer who I hadn't had the pleasure of meeting yet.

My next job was to get rid of the cigarettes. I didn't think I would have any problem in doing that as cigarettes were rationed and hard to get.

In the first three pubs I tried the landlords weren't interested even though I wasn't asking the full price. Paddy was with me and each pub we went into we had a swift half so it was costing us money. Except the Grapes, which was a Tetley's house, so we had pints.

We decided to try the Huntsman and if we had no luck there I would share them out with the lads that smoked and put my loss down to the cruel school of experience.

Just before we reached the Huntsman, Paddy noticed a little tobacconist shop on a side street. The lady in the shop asked us if we had just come back from abroad and said if we had she could let us have twenty each. I explained to her we had just come back from abroad, neither of us smoked and we had some cigarettes to sell. She bought them from us and insisted on giving us the full retail price.

It just went to show that all the ladies in Blackpool were not like the one in Crystal Road.

After selling the cigarettes we had a walk on the sea front and had a look in one or two shops which was quite a novelty to us.

In a Boots store an old lady came up to us and asked what the medal ribbon on my tunic was for. I told her it was the Africa Star and Eighth Army clasp. She gave us ten shillings each (50p) saying we had done our bit. I didn't know which bit she meant but we were moved to think that someone thought well of us. Maybe her husband had been in the First World War. Ten shillings was more than a day's pay.

We had fish and chips and another walk on the promenade. It seemed strange to see lots of people on holiday at the height of the war. Not that they didn't deserve a week's break, as many of them would have been working twelve hours a day for seven days a week. I sometimes thought we were better off in the forces. Except that they were getting a pound a day for making bullets and we were getting a few shillings a day for stopping bullets. That is if you were conscientious and did your job right.

I was beginning to worry about Jean as I hadn't written to her since we left Egypt and none of her letters had caught up with us yet. So I decided the first thing I would do after my tea was to write to her and tell her I was back in England.

Since our last night on the ship we hadn't had any sleep so I was feeling a bit jaded and I suggested to Paddy that we made our way to the Central Pier, find a bench to rest on and watch the world go by.

Just past the lifeboat station Paddy said, 'Look at him.' At the other side of the tramlines was an RAF sergeant. He was as drunk as a handcart and staggering all over the place. All of a sudden he set off across the tramlines going two steps forward and one step backwards. A tram was coming towards him at full speed and when he got to the middle of the line he turned to look at it coming towards him. Blackpool trams came to a little point at the front and it hit him dead centre. He went up into the air and landed at our feet which were about ten yards from where the tram had hit him. His head looked as if it had been chopped down the middle with an axe.

Some of the holidaymakers who were passing by ran away and I could hear women screaming.

There was one man that came to us and suggested we carried him into the lifeboat station. He looked to be in his fifties, maybe he had been in the First World War and had seen plenty of this kind of thing.

The man took one arm, I took the other and Paddy took his feet.

In the lifeboat station there was a first aid cubicle with a bunk in it on which we laid him. There was a St. John's nurse in attendance who went a bit pale but managed to keep her composure. She rang for the police and an ambulance and asked us to stay with her until they arrived.

We stayed and I wish we hadn't, as much of our time in the following days in Blackpool was taken up by having to go to various places to answer questions concerning the accident. First it was the police, then the tramways department, the RAF and the inquest.

Paddy and I talked it over and decided we would tell the same tale at each place, which was that we heard a bump and the next thing we saw was the sergeant's body at our feet.

Our reasoning was that if we told the truth and said the sergeant had been drunk his dependants would not have been compensated, and if we had said what speed the tram was going the driver would have been in trouble, so we stuck to our story.

Teatime at the digs was at five o'clock and the landlady had let us know that if we weren't there at dead on five we wouldn't be getting any. So it was dead on five when the four of us sat down at the table furthest away from the window and the holiday-makers. A young girl waitress brought us our meal of Spam, chips and beans with a cup of tea. I couldn't help noticing that the holidaymakers were having soup then chicken, roast potatoes, Yorkshire pudding and vegetables, with cream cakes for dessert.

It was no wonder she had been so keen to get hold of our ration cards when we first arrived.

I thought at the time that it wouldn't have been a bad place to stay, unless you were in uniform.

After tea I wrote two letters, one to Jean and the other to home. When I had finished writing the letters I lay down to have a sleep intending to wake up around nine o'clock and go for a drink. By this time my three pals were all fast asleep and when I did wake up it was too late to go for a drink as the pubs would have been closed. The other three were all snoring their heads off. With me not having my quota of beer I had a bad nightmare, it woke the others and caused a lot of cursing and swearing.

On the second night Paddy and I decided to go to the first house at the tower circus. We got seats in the balcony. The tiers of the seats were so steep that our feet were on a level with the heads of two elderly ladies sat in front of us.

When the elephants came on to do their act the ladies started going on about the smell. Even after the elephants had gone and clowns came on they were still saying, 'I can still smell those bloody elephants.'

Paddy and I had both bought a pair of black cotton socks in Egypt before we left and except for when we were on the ship we were still wearing them. I nudged Paddy and pointed to our feet, he got into a fit of laughing. It was a good job the clowns were still doing their act for if they hadn't been I think we would have been asked to leave. He was still laughing his head off when we got settled down in the Grapes for a drink.

On parade on the fourth morning the sergeant marched us off to the football ground and in we went once again to the big area beneath the stand.

The tired looking WAAFs were still there; we queued up again at the tables and were given leave passes, ration cards and travel warrants for three weeks. We were also told that we would be notified where to report back to whilst we were on leave.

On the train to Bradford I met an old pal of mine, we had grown up together in Royd Street, his name was Harry Ingham. He told me he had just done three years in Freetown working on the guns on the Sunderland flying boats.

Freetown was once known as the white man's grave due to the nasty diseases that could be caught in such places. Because of this it was like Iraq in that it was a three year station, unlike the Middle East and India which were four years.

On arriving at Exchange Station in Bradford Harry suggested that instead of lugging our kit on and off trams it would be better if we shared a taxi. I thought it was a good idea except that it was five pence a mile.

It was the first time I had been in a taxi in England so it was a bit of a novelty and in any case my mother, my dad and sister had moved from Royd Street to a little side scullery house in a back yard somewhere at the bottom of St. Stephen's Road. I hadn't a clue where it was but I felt sure the taxi driver would know.

At Royd Street there were banners across the road saying 'Welcome Home Harry'. Seeing my old surroundings gave me a deep feeling of nostalgia.

I asked the taxi driver if he knew 256 St. Stephen's Road and he did. He helped me get my kit out of the boot and I was home sweet home at last.

The house was up a passage and when I got to the door it was open and all was quiet inside, so just in case I was at the wrong house I had a look inside. There before me was the sideboard with the large mirror on the back and the familiar looking couch, table and chairs so in I went.

I could hear a noise upstairs. There was a door into the kitchen on my right and another door on the back wall in the corner that

I gathered would be the staircase leading up to the bedrooms.

I opened the door and called, 'Hello.'

My mother's voice called back, 'Who is it?'

I said, 'It's Jack,' and my mother said:

'I'm making the beds. I will be down in a minute,' and that was my homecoming.

My mother took one look at me and said, 'You look thin.' I hadn't been what you would call fat the last time she had seen me and I expect I did look on the scrawny side as I had lost one and a half stone since then.

While my mother was making a pot of tea in the kitchen I had a good look at myself in the sideboard mirror. I saw a spotty face with brown patches here and there. Where there were no brown patches it was a kind of a putty colour and my eyes looked like piss holes in the snow.

It was the first time I had seen myself in a mirror for a long time as I had been using the bottom of my mess tin polished up a bit for shaving and it was not a pretty sight.

As we were drinking the tea I asked my mother why they had moved from the three bedroomed house in Royd Street to this one with only two bedrooms, for I was wondering where I was going to sleep. I had worked out my mother and my dad would be in the big bedroom and my sister in the small one. It took a while for her to answer me. When she did she said, 'When you had been away such a long time we didn't think you would be coming back.'

Whether they thought I was going to get killed or married I didn't like to ask so the sleeping arrangements were that I slept on the couch. I tried it on the first night but didn't like it and moved on to the floor. It was back to square one except now I had a cushion for a pillow instead of a life jacket.

I gave her the ration card and money for the next three weeks which was gratefully accepted.

We sat chatting for a while and she seemed upset that our poor Harry had been posted to Dunoon in Scotland and she always had to send him money for cigarettes. I didn't bother asking what had happened to the money from my ill-gotten gains that I had sent from time to time but I guessed that with there being a greyhound racing track at Dunoon it had finished up there. When it came to gambling our poor Harry couldn't help himself.

At tea time my dad and Agnes came home from work. Dad was

over the moon that I had got back safe and sound. Agnes wanted to know all the countries that I had been to. I don't know to this day if she believed me, it did seem a lot even to me.

After tea I had a wash and shave, spruced myself up and went to Jean's house.

I knew that in all probability Jean wouldn't be home but I would find out from her mother and her dad when she would be.

It gave me a funny feeling when I saw the house and gas lamp outside where we used to have our kiss and cuddle in what seemed now to be far off happy days.

George and Lily seemed pleased to see me until I told them I had been at Blackpool for four days. Then they were not so pleased, for Jean had only gone back off leave the night before. He said that if I had let them know I was in Blackpool he would have brought her to see me, so I had not got off to a good start at the Robinsons.

After tea and biscuits and a chat things got more friendly. George said I should send a telegram to Jean as soon as the post office opened in the morning and tell her I was home.

Leaving the house I walked down Gain Lane and called in at the Junction pub for a pint and to ponder about what a mess I had made of my homecoming so far.

After walking two and a half miles home I lay down on the floor and fell asleep wondering what the next few days had in store for me.

I slept through without a nightmare and at nine o'clock next morning I was at the post office to send the telegram to Jean. I had never sent a telegram before so the lady at the post office had to help me with it.

I got a reply from Jean saying she would be on the train from London that evening.

Back home my mother had had a letter from my brother Harry saying he had no money or cigarettes and that he was going to be sent to France in the near future.

He had remustered from being a driver and was now a cook in the Royal Service Corps.

My mother was upset and kept talking about her brother Willie who had been killed in France in the First World War.

I went to Exchange Station to find out the time of the train from London that evening which was at six o'clock.

In the afternoon I went and sat on a park bench and watched the old men playing bowls. It was difficult to imagine that three hundred miles away young men were being slaughtered like sheep.

Six o'clock couldn't come too soon and I was there on the platform with my penny platform ticket.

The train was late and there was no sign of Jean.

On the train arrival board it said that the next train from London would be expected at nine o'clock so I had three hours to wait.

Having three hours to kill I decided to go and see my Aunt Agnes and Uncle Willie.

They were pleased to see me and after tea and cakes Willie asked me to go with him for a pint. I politely declined as I didn't want to meet Jean smelling of beer and still I knew that if I didn't have a drink it was an even money bet I would have the nightmare.

The nine o'clock train was also late and I was beginning to wonder if it would turn up at all, for although the bombing had eased off a lot there was still a chance of one dropping on the lines near London.

When it did arrive I was on the platform eagerly watching the carriage doors opening.

All of a sudden I saw her walking down the platform towards me. She was in uniform with her gas mask slung on her shoulder. As she got near I thought that she looked tired and sad.

Our meeting wasn't like I had seen on the films where they run towards each other and get entangled in a long embrace. She just looked at me and said, 'Hello Jack.' I felt I had to do something so I put my arms round her and gave her a big hug.

On our way to the Thornbury tram we seemed to be at a loss what to say to each other and like her father she was annoyed at me being at Blackpool when she had been on leave and said how difficult it had been getting a seventy-two hour pass when she had just got back from leave.

When we got off the tram it struck me I should have got a taxi. I was beginning to think that I couldn't do right for doing wrong.

At Jean's house her mother and father were ready for going to bed but Lily kindly made us a cup of tea and a sandwich.

There seemed to be a coolness between us that I thought may

be caused through us not seeing each other for a long time; we were both feeling a bit strange or shy.

At one part in our conversation she said I looked different from when I had gone away. She didn't have to tell me whether I looked better or worse.

She told me what she had been doing and where she had been and how marvellous the dancing was at the Hammersmith Palais de Dance.

She asked me what I had been doing and I didn't feel like going into detail. I said it had been hot and dusty.

The time came for me to go home and after a kiss and a cuddle off I went.

On my way back to West Bowling our meeting gave me plenty of food for thought, so my walk home didn't seem far.

Jean had told me not to call the next day saying she would call for me about lunchtime.

The next day she called for me as arranged. It was lovely weather and Jean suggested we walk over Baildon Moor. So we went on the tram to Saltaire, walked up Shipley Glen and on to the moors.

Once up there we sat a while but our conversation never seemed to get round to the future, and when I tried Jean abruptly changed the subject.

We went back to her house for tea so that she could get changed into civvies and go dancing at the Ideal.

At the interval I asked if it was all right if I got a pass-out and went for a drink in the Red Lion next door. Ladies were not allowed pass-outs.

When I got back she was dancing with a sailor and looked to be having a good laugh.

I was having a bit of a struggle with my footwork and Jean remarked that my dancing hadn't improved much since I went away. The only thing I could think of saying was that no one had been giving dancing lessons in the desert.

We spent the next day together without any kind of progress in our love making and in the afternoon I went to see her off on the train for she was due back in camp at midnight.

After the first two weeks of my leave I received a letter from the RAF together with a travel warrant telling me to report to RAF station Fiskerton on the ninth of July.

All it said about Fiskerton was that it was somewhere in Lincolnshire. All I could do was get on the train and let them sort it out for me.

The train stopped for a while at Doncaster. I opened the carriage window to get a breath of fresh air and there staggering along the platform were Joe Merrin and Frank Taylor with kitbags on their shoulders. Frank had the nickname of Abdul because he was a bit dark skinned. It was good to see them, for although they had never been on my post on the wireless unit they had always been good pals.

I gave them a shout and they joined me. They were on their way to Fiskerton same as me.

Joe was married and came from Derby. The first thing I asked him after we got settled down was how he had gone on with his sex whilst he had been on leave. He said that if there was anything better he would spend all his wages on it.

The reason for me asking him was that when we were near Tripoli, which seemed ages ago, Joe got sand behind his foreskin and got a disease called banalities or something like that. It meant him having to go into the hospital at Tripoli and be circumcised – a nasty operation for an adult and it took a long time for it to heal up. Most likely because of the conditions he was living under at the time. After that Joe used to worry about it being all right if and when he ever got back to his wife.

Abdul was a booze artist and would drink anything except water so I wouldn't be short of company.

We talked it over and decided when we got to Lincoln we would have to find a bus or a train to take us to Fiskerton and if there were no buses or trains we would have to hitch-hike.

At Lincoln there was a surprise waiting for us in the shape of a corporal who saw us as soon as we alighted on to the platform with all our gear. He came up to us and said, 'Hello, are you the lads for Fiskerton?'

Outside the station was a Humber Snipe shooting brake that took us to the guardroom at Fiskerton. On our way the corporal told us that the station warrant officer was expecting us and it was him that had arranged the transport. After the three ton Fords we had been used to in the desert it made us feel like royalty.

After we booked in at the guardroom, the SP sergeant took us to a small cluster of huts at the bottom side of the main road that went through the camp.

Our three beds were already made up. He told us to put our kit on the bed and we could sort it out later. He then took us to the cookhouse for a late tea which had been arranged for us.

Our tea was sausage, mash and beans with jam roly-poly for afters with seconds if we wanted and a lovely pot of tea.

We asked the sergeant what the beer was like in the NAAFI and he told us it was the same as in the sergeants' mess just not so good. The beer at the pub in the village that I think was called the Royal Oak was all right when they had any and if they sold out of beer they always had cider. I only tried the cider once and I had a headache for two days.

All this had been arranged by the SWO to whom we had been instructed to report at nine o'clock the following morning.

That night we went to the NAAFI and had a few pints and as the sergeant had said the beer wasn't anything to crack on about. Abdul remarked that there wasn't such a thing as bad beer, just that some was worse than others.

We sat on our own at a table like new boys are apt to do and chatted about the good times and the bad times on our past units and wondered where all our old pals had finished up.

It always surprised me how you could eat, drink, sleep and wander about the world with lads who you got to know better than your own brother and then never see them again.

I noticed in our conversation that my folly at the farmhouse in Tunisia was never mentioned. So it looked as if my comrades on our post had kept their promise and not spread it around the unit.

At one part of the night, when it was my turn to pay, Abdul went to the bar with me to help carry the pints. The girl behind the counter was a bonny looking girl with a Yorkshire accent. She asked me what the silver rosette was for on our African Star medal ribbon. Before I could give her an answer Abdul said that it was for fighting in North Africa. She said, 'What? With guns?' and he replied, 'No, with washing up mops.' She blushed and went away looking a bit embarrassed and by the look on Abdul's face I think he knew he had said the wrong thing. But like a poem we learned at school about when words are spoken, it is like an arrow shot from a bow and there is no way of bringing them back.

After a good breakfast the next morning we went up to the SWO's office. We were a bit early and he wasn't there but there was an LAC (Leading Aircraftsman) sat twiddling his thumbs. He told us that the SWO would be there shortly and I said, 'Don't call me Shorty.' He told us we had better watch our P's and Q's as the Warrant Officer was a stickler for discipline.

When the SWO did enter the office the three of us sprang to attention. He smiled and said, 'Sit down lads. There is no need for all that.' The LAC clerk was sat behind his table with a grin of satisfaction on his face knowing that he had put the wind up us.

He didn't grin for long when the SWO told him to go to the bicycle shed and tell the corporal there to get three bikes ready for dinnertime.

He asked us our names, we told him our surnames but it was Christian names he wanted to know.

He introduced himself as Mr Holmes (SWOs were always addressed as Mister).

He seemed a nice old man and went on to tell us that we had done our bit and we could get settled in and have it easy for a while. He told us to come back at dinnertime to collect our bikes and then in the afternoon we could have a ride around the camp and get to know our way about.

He told us that he was forty-eight years old and he had been in the First World War in the Royal Flying Corps before it was changed to the RAF. I could tell that he had been in the first war by his medal ribbons. Twenty-eight years seemed a long time for anyone to spend in the forces. When he had asked my age he told me that he had a daughter in the WAAFs the same age.

If this was life in the RAF in England it would do for me.

When we had drawn our bikes and had our dinner we had a ride around the camp.

On the airfield there were a lot of Lancaster bombers being loaded with bombs by the armourers. Some of the bombs were the size of dustbins and to make them bigger they were bolting two together. It made me wonder how they got off the ground carrying all that weight. It was a frightening sight but not as frightening as it would be for the people at the receiving end.

A few days passed by and the weather was fine so it gave us a chance to go for cycle rides and enjoy our new surroundings.

The bonny girl in the canteen gave me a jar of Brylcreme and a bar of chocolate. Abdul said, 'She must fancy you.' I thought it was more likely that she felt sorry for me as I don't think my reunion with Jean had done my inferiority complex a lot of good.

A day later I got a letter from Jean asking me if I had got settled in on my new camp etc. I noticed that it started off with 'My dear Jack,' when before it had always been 'My own darling Jack,'.

I knew then the writing was on the wall. I felt as if the future had fallen out of my life and I would have to get things sorted out one way or the other. So the next morning when I went to see Mr Holmes I asked him if I could have a word with him in private.

He listened to me and when I finished he said these things happen in wartime. The best advice he could give was for him to give me a forty-eight hour pass to go to Halton where Jean was stationed and take the bull by the horns.

The next morning I was on my way. I hitch-hiked as far as Bedford where I got bed and breakfast and took local trains to Wendover the next morning.

That night I sat in a pub going over in my mind what I would say on my meeting with Jean.

I found out the next day that I had had no need to bother as it had all been worked out for me.

Halton camp was only a short walk from Wendover and I arrived there about lunchtime.

After making a few enquiries I eventually found her in the canteen with a friend she introduced as Jackie. Jean asked me if I would like a cup of tea and something to eat, I offered to go for it but she insisted on going.

While Jean was at the counter being served Jackie said Jean seemed surprised to see me and then after a pause added, 'You are not the only one you know.'

I knew straight away what she meant and why Jean had insisted going for the tea; she couldn't face up to telling me herself.

I didn't say a word about it when we said goodbye but I did notice there were tears in her eyes.

Afterwards, I thought I should have talked to her and tried to do something about it.

On my way back to Fiskerton my mind was in a quandary and at one stage I was thinking that with my nightmares and drinking it was maybe for the best. Then I got to thinking that out of respect and love for her I had always been satisfied with a kiss and a cuddle until the big day when we were married.

Maybe it wasn't enough for her? So when I had got over feeling sorry for myself I vowed I would never fall madly in love or get emotionally attached to anyone again as it usually finishes up in heartache.

Before the train arrived at Lincoln I made an effort to calm myself down and made up my mind that in future when it came to affairs with the opposite sex it would be a jar of hair cream on my head, down to the dance hall and straight at it.

The next day back at Fiskerton Mr Holmes asked me how I had gone on. When I told him he said the same as I had been thinking, maybe it was for the best.

One morning we went to report at nine o'clock and he asked if we would do a little job for him. Even though he asked we knew we couldn't refuse, but being asked was much better than being given an order.

Some of the general duty lads had started making a cinema in one of the empty huts on the camp. The little job Mr Holmes had for us was to go with a wagon and driver to a cinema in Mansfield that was closing down where they were selling the seats off at five shillings (25p) each. He had ordered one hundred seats that were to be paid for out of PSI money (a percentage of the profits from the NAAFI). He gave me the money and off we went.

When we found the cinema the man in charge was going for his dinner and said if we wanted we could go with him.

I had a better idea and told him if he didn't mind we would sooner load up and be on our way back to Fiskerton. I gave him the money and we got cracking as fast as we could. We managed to get a hundred and thirty seats into the back of the wagon. The driver grumbled saying, 'the springs won't stand the weight.'

On the return journey all four of us had to squash into the front of the wagon with Abdul sat on the engine cover which, judging by his continual moaning, must have got rather hot, and I sat on Joe's knees.

When we got back to camp and Mr Holmes found we had purloined thirty seats extra you would have thought he had won the pools. He couldn't stop telling us that when he first set eyes on us he knew he had got three good lads. Which made me wonder if he was paying us a compliment or if he was saying we looked like villains.

A day or two after our Mansfield trip he asked us if we would like to do some painting. I told him Abdul and I had been apprentice decorators in civvy street and Joe had been a window cleaner so a spot of painting would be no problem.

The job was to redecorate the NAAFI and with us being the tradesmen we would choose the colour scheme. We went to look at the job and see how much paint and materials we would require.

The civilian clerk of works was to fix us up with paint but he was short of brushes and sandpaper so Mr Holmes suggested that with Joe living at Derby he would know best where to buy the things we needed. He gave us passes for forty-eight hours and more PSI money and off we went to Derby.

Joe was to spend the night at home with his wife who was living with Joe's mother, dad and granddad. Abdul and I were to stay at the YMCA but when we got to Joe's house his mother insisted we should stay with them.

Abdul and I tossed a coin to see who slept on the settee and who slept in the double bed with Joe's granddad. I lost and finished up in bed with his granddad in the attic.

After tea we all went to the local cinema to see 'Goodbye Mr Chips' which was a silly thing for me to do, because with me not having my ration of medicine I had a nightmare which awakened granddad much to his annoyance as he had to be up at six to go to work at the Ceylonese factory.

When we got back to Fiskerton to start on the decorating I found the only paint the clerk of works had was white. I went to Lincoln to find a decorators and got some stainers. I managed to get ochre, Venetian red and Prussian blue. So with a little ochre added to the white we could get cream. Ochre and a bit of blue would give a nice delicate green and so on with the other colours. When the job was completed we finished up with a pleasant scheme of pastel colours.

When I was in the NAAFI painting I plucked up courage and asked the bonny girl from Barnsley if she fancied going for a drink with me on her night off. Without any hesitation she said she thought I would never ask. On her next night off we went to the pub in the village. She seemed a nice girl, her name was Irene. We talked about home and her work in the canteen and had a drink or two.

I told her that with me being away from England for a long time and not having much experience with girls she may find me a bit backward at coming forward.

She gathered what I meant and told me she would show me how to go on, and she did with a bonus in a field behind a hedge on our way back to camp.

Irene and I went out together on her nights off until I left Fiskerton. When I did leave I promised to write to her but didn't; I still had Jean on my mind and what might have been.

One night I had a really bad nightmare and woke all the lads in the hut up and they were not pleased.

The LAC runner or clerk, or whatever his job was, slept in the hut and must have mentioned it to Mr Holmes the next morning for when we reported to him at nine o'clock he dismissed Joe and Abdul and asked me to stay back as he wanted to have a word with me.

He suggested I should go and see the medical officer and maybe he could arrange to get me some counselling. I agreed and he rang the MO who said he would see me right away.

He seemed a decent enough chap and on looking at my medical records before him he said, 'I see here you had a problem with loss of memory when you were at Beirut.'

He talked to me at length about traumas and nightmares etc.

I didn't tell him the reason for my nightmares as I felt so guilty about it that I had made up my mind never to tell anyone. After talking to me for a while longer he said he would arrange for me to visit a hospital to see a psychiatrist. What he didn't tell me was that it was in a mental hospital.

The very next morning the sergeant from the MT section came with the Humber Snipe and told me to pack my small kit and away we went.

The so-called hospital was a big house in its own grounds. By what I could make out it was somewhere between Gainsborough and Retford.

Once I got settled in and talking to some of the lads I gathered I would only be there for a few days to be assessed and if they judged me to be proper doolally I would be transferred to a big place nearby. Once they got you in there, there was no telling when they would let you out and that was frightening to say the least.

Besides being frightening I found the place disgusting as most of the lads in there were sergeant pilots or air gunners. Some of the pilots had been in the Battle of Britain and the gunners had all been on bombing raids over Germany. They were nearly all suffering from nervous breakdowns which the clever people diagnosed as LMF (lacking in moral fibre).

How people in authority could brand these men with words like that, labelling them as cowards, was to me beyond belief and this coming from people who were supposed to be intelligent. Although it was better than the First World War, as the dunder-heads who were in charge then would have had them shot at dawn.

On the third morning in there I had to see the trick cyclist. He was a bored looking flying officer without wings and told me to sit down. All the time I was there he stood towering over me. He said he had been looking at my records and could well understand my problem, as it was a common enough complaint with men who had seen active service.

I told him the only way I could be sure I didn't have a nightmare was to drink a fair amount of alcohol before I went to bed. He said this was no remedy but didn't tell me what his remedy was, that is if he had one, which I doubted very much.

It made me think there are easier ways of making a living in wartime than fighting the enemy or working twelve hours a day on munitions.

The next day I was on my way back to Fiskerton with a feeling of relief at having left the mental hospital.

This is the first time since then that I have disclosed to anyone about the mental hospital, because in those days the stigma of such a place was tantamount to being in prison. We should be thankful that these days things have changed for the better.

When I went to see Mr Holmes the next morning he asked me how I had gone on and then told me a pal of his who was the SWO at a bomber station called Fulbeck had been in touch with him and asked him if he had a corporal to spare as he was in need of a disciplinary NCO. If I fancied the job he was willing to let me go, as I was always ready for a change I said yes.

The next day I packed my kit, said farewell to Joe and Abdul and off I went again with the MT sergeant to Fulbeck which wasn't very far away. It was just one of the bomber stations scattered all over Lincolnshire in those days.

On arriving at Fulbeck I left my kit in the service police guardroom at the main entrance to the camp and told the corporal on duty who I was and why I was there.

He took me to the SWO's office, which was the next building on the site camp.

The corporal left me standing at the door, it had 'Station Warrant Officer' on it in bold block lettering making it look somewhat formidable so I knocked and waited.

A tall leading aircraftsman with the African Star on his chest answered the door. He was the warrant officer's runner and his only duties were keeping the office tidy, lighting the stove before we got there in the morning and bringing tea and rock buns from the NAAFI at break time.

I only ever knew him as Lofty and he was slightly disabled. He had been a dispatch rider in North Africa and had had one of his elbows shot off which gave him permission to wear a wound stripe on his sleeve of which he was very proud.

I went in, stood to attention and said, 'Corporal Davidson, come to report sir.'

He was sat behind his desk filling in some form or other. After a while he put down his pen, looked up at me, cocked his head to one side and said, 'So you are Dave. I have heard a lot about you.' I worried if what he had heard was good or bad.

There was another desk with a chair by the window; when I say desk it was a trestle table with a blanket on it.

He told me to sit down and said he would put me in the picture regarding my duties. He then told Lofty that it was break time and off he went on his bicycle with his tea tin. No money changed hands so I gathered that with the SWO being the king of the camp we didn't pay for our tea and rock buns.

His name was Frank Taylor which was a coincidence as that was also Abdul's proper name. He told me that I had no need to address him as sir unless there were other people about; so it was Frank and Dave.

My duties were to be with him each morning to march defaulters into the Commanding Officer's office to receive their punishment and to make sure I knocked their caps off as they went in.

I found some of the crimes they committed were so funny that it was difficult not to laugh.

There was one lad on a charge for urinating in a corporal's ear when the corporal was asleep.

There was a WAAF from the MT section who was on a charge for leaving her wagon door wide open and getting it knocked off by another wagon. The trouble was she had done it twice before! The main of the charges were for coming in late and being absent without leave.

My duty on some mornings was to take a group of aircrew cadets for rifle and foot drill. On other mornings Frank and I would go off on our bicycles to inspect the cookhouse and living quarters. I had to have my little notebook ready to make a note of anything that wasn't up to scratch.

When we were inspecting the cookhouse the cookhouse sergeant always accompanied us and after a while I hit on a ploy which was if Frank said, 'That sink is dirty. Corporal, make a note of it.' I would say 'Maybe they have only just finished using it sir and have not got around to cleaning it yet.'

This put me in the sergeant's good books and enabled me to get a good feed in the cookhouse on nights when I had my beer in the NAAFI instead of going to the pub at Metheringham or Brant Broughton.

Frank never mentioned it but I think that he knew what I was up to.

He became a good pal after a while; he had been in the RAF for fourteen years and was looking forward to finishing his time and going out on full pension. He had done three years in Iraq before the war so we had plenty to talk about. When he had been a sergeant drill instructor at Blackpool he had married in haste and regretted it.

One morning he came back from the admin section and said, 'We have been given a rotten job to do.' I took it to be the royal 'we' which meant that I would have to do it.

It turned out that a Spitfire had nose dived into a ploughed field about twenty-five miles from Fulbeck.

This happened quite often, for sometimes when a pilot took a plane into a dive he would black out from the pressure and not be capable of pulling out of the dive.

Someone with a warped mind had suggested that I took six of the young cadets to dig it out and get what was left of the pilot's body. Maybe they thought that it would give the cadets a taste of what they had let themselves in for.

A WAAF driver took us to the site in a three-ton wagon along with picks, shovels, a wheelbarrow, a big kettle and haversack rations.

Arrangements had been made at the farm in which field the plane had crashed in to boil our water and provide somewhere to sleep.

The farmer, who sounded as if he was blaming me for the plane crashing in his field, was anything but pleasant.

When I asked the farmer's wife to boil some water for us she said that she hadn't time to be boiling water for the likes of us lot and why didn't we light a fire, like boy scouts do. I had already asked the farmer where we could sleep and he had shown me a draughty old barn stacked up with bales of hay.

What annoyed me the most was that they would most likely be getting compensated for looking after us.

I decided not to bother the farmer and his wife any more as I never did like begging.

The village was only a five to ten minute walk so when we needed water two of the cadets went with the kettle and got it filled at the police station.

We built a fireplace with stones, collected firewood and sat round the fire. The only problem I had was getting the cadets to leave the fire and get on with the digging as it was bitterly cold.

That night we got settled down in the barn on the bales of hay with just the light from a hurricane lamp.

I had no sooner nodded off to sleep when I was woken by the lads who seemed to be excited about something or other. The barn was running with rats, they were all over the place putting a stop to any of us having a night's sleep.

To get back to the job we were there for. I had marked out a seven or eight foot square where I estimated the cockpit of the aircraft would be with what was left of the pilot in it. I hadn't told the young lads that all we would find were bits and pieces of him.

Later that day a sergeant and a driver turned up with a wooden box to put his remains in. I told them to come back in two or three days as we had hardly got through the layer of frozen soil which was about six inches thick. They looked as if they were glad to be on their way.

Later that day things took a turn for the better. When the lads had gone down to the police house to fill the kettle for our morning brew they had told the police sergeant about the barn, the rats and the cold.

In the afternoon the sergeant came up to the farm to see me. He said he had found a better place for us to sleep and would I go with him and have a look at it.

It was a large upstairs room in a building adjoining the village pub. It was where the home guard and various village groups had their meetings. I thanked him and said it would do fine.

There was a fireplace in the room and when we got back at teatime there was paper, firewood, a bin full of coal and a flush toilet in the corner of the room.

Even after all this luxury one of the posh cadets asked me where he could get washed.

Once we had got through the frozen six inches of soil digging became much easier but it amazed me how far the plane had gone into the ground on impact. The frost must have come on the night after it had crashed.

That same afternoon, just before it got dark, two American officers turned up to see what we were doing. They said they had heard about the crash but didn't realise how near it was to their camp which was about a mile away among some trees. They asked us what we were doing about our meals. When I told them, they insisted we went and had meals at their camp, which we did and the food was great.

It took nearly two more days before we got to the nasty part. When we did it was just the same as the crash I had been involved with in the mountains near Beirut. The pilot along with the aircraft was all in bits mixed up one with the other.

The first bit I pulled out was the pilot's helmet with part of his head in it. When I passed it up to one of the cadets he went as white as a sheet and dropped it; one of the others was sick.

It wasn't long before we had enough bits of body to justify a funeral and the rest of the aircraft I left for a recovery unit to deal with.

I wondered later how many of the cadets would still have the ambition to become pilots.

Not long after I had got settled in again on my comfy little job at the SWO's office a signal came through that I was to go on a

NCO's course at Butlins Holiday Camp at Filey in Yorkshire.

I was there for three weeks being taught what I had been doing for the last four years.

Little did I know what the course was preparing me for, but I found out a few months later. It was now getting on towards Christmas and the weather was turning much colder which came as a shock after my spell in the warmer climes.

Christmas came along as it always does at this time of the year and Frank said I could have a week's leave. So I went home to Bradford.

My parents were glad to see me and I got settled in sleeping on the couch again and enjoying home comforts for seven days.

Each night I managed to get a few pints down to make me sleep and on two of the days I went for walks on the moors with my dad. On a couple of nights I went to the Ideal Ballroom at Bankfoot but it wasn't the same now there was no Jean to greet me. At the end of the leave I felt glad I was going back to camp.

At Fulbeck there was a barn positioned about halfway round the airfield where the sanitary squad (half a dozen lads that cleaned the latrines each morning) had been feeding ten geese up for Christmas. These geese had been fed with scraps from the cookhouse since summer. The geese were supposed to be for Christmas dinner but when I asked the corporal in charge of the squad what they tasted like, he said, 'I don't know as four of them have gone to the officers' mess, two to the sergeants' mess and the remaining four are still in the barn.'

There was a flight sergeant Parry – I never knew what his job was except that he spent a lot of time helping the entertainments officer and now and then he would call into the office for a chat. The day after I found out about the geese he called in to ask me if I would do a few posters for a dance in the officers' mess. When I told him about the geese he was as annoyed as I was. He said, 'If I knew how to kill them I would go to the barn one dark night and get one for my lady friend at Brant Broughton.'

Fortunately Frank and Lofty were out of the office at the time so the conversation was just between the two of us.

I asked him if he had a sharp knife and he said, 'I have a sheath knife I've kept with me since my Boy Scout days.' He seemed to take it for granted that I was going with him on the dirty deed and I had already made my mind up that if he was having one so was I.

We planned to do it on the following Friday night hoping that Frank would let me go home for the weekend.

The following Friday, at around eight o'clock, we were passing the guardroom on our bicycles. It was bitterly cold so the service policeman that should have been on the gate was nowhere to be seen, he was most likely warming his toes in front of the guardroom stove.

There were no opps. on that night so luckily for us no one was about and as we pedalled through the snow around the perimeter it was deadly quiet.

The barn was unlocked so in we went. I had had the presence of mind to take a torch with us. When the geese heard us they started shuffling about and squawking but when I switched my torch on they all stood stock still. Most likely they were dazzled by the light.

In those few seconds I managed to grab the one nearest to me and they all started running about and squawking again.

I got hold of its beak with its neck between my legs and its body behind me. The flight sergeant now had the torch and was just stood there with me frantically telling him to give me the knife. He was fumbling about inside his greatcoat until he eventually found it. After asking my helper to take the knife out its sheath he gave it to me. I started cutting away at the goose's neck until its head came off.

While I was doing this the flight sergeant had pulled himself together and grabbed another goose that I dealt with in the same way. Meanwhile there was pandemonium going on with the two that were left. Maybe they thought they were on death row.

After we got over our panic and excitement we put the dead geese into a couple of spare kitbags we had brought with us.

It was blowing a blizzard when we got outside and was covering our tracks up straight away; it looked as if lady luck was still with us.

Flight sergeant Parry went to his billet, I went back to mine and put my ill-gotten goods in the cupboard where we kept the cleaning tackle.

There was still time to have a pint or two so I went trudging through the snow to the NAAFI and tried to work out what I was going to say to Frank the next morning.

In the light of day I wondered if I had done the right thing, as

I would have to tell him about my caper in order to get a forty-eight hour pass.

I got to the office early and Lofty had just lit the fire, so when I saw Frank passing the window I asked him to go to the orderly room to see if there was any mail or messages. I knew he would be a while as he always had a chat with the girls that worked in there and it would give me time to tell Frank what I had done.

After he had kicked the snow off his boots he came in muttering obscenities about the weather. He was in a foul mood which wasn't going to make my position any easier. I took the bull by the horns and told him what I had been up to the night before without mentioning the flight sergeant.

He went blue in the face, told me I was stark raving mad and that it was no wonder they had had me in the funny farm. This upset me, as I didn't know he knew about that little episode.

He kept going on, saying the police would come and he was unable to tell lies without it showing on his face.

One consolation was that all the time he was raving on he was making a forty-eight hour pass out for me. Finally he said, 'I don't know why I am giving you this when you only came back off leave last week. So take it to the orderly room, get it stamped, get out of my sight and don't forget to take that bloody goose with you.'

The goose had frozen solid in the night even though it had been in the cupboard.

I hitch-hiked to Newark and got a penny platform ticket (a trick used by a lot of servicemen as they didn't have ticket collectors on the trains in those days). Soon I was on the next train to Bradford, but I got off the train at St. Dunstan's, the last stop before Bradford. I climbed over the railings as it was pitch dark by the time I got there; it just goes to show that even the blackout had its advantages.

My mother and my dad were surprised to see me with me only having been back a week.

I told them that I had won the goose in a raffle. My mother couldn't believe it as she had dreamt that I had won a raffle only two nights before, she must have been with me in spirit in the barn.

All this pleased her, for dreaming, reading teacups and fortune telling were her favourite pastimes even though she was a devout Roman Catholic and the Church frowned on such activities.

I didn't get a chance to taste the goose, as it hadn't thawed by the time I had to go back to Fulbeck.

The next time my dad wrote to me he said the goose was lovely and there had been plenty of grease on it to save for rubbing on their chests in the winter months to come.

Frank was still in a bad mood when I got back and kept going on about the police questioning him.

At the finish of it all the police concluded it must have been a fox owing to the fact that foxes usually bite the heads off their prey before taking the body away. What beat me about this theory was how the fox had opened and closed the barn door. I looked on this as a bit of lazy detective work on their part!

Things carried on nicely through the winter months. I drilled the cadets, held the defaulters' parade, had good food, kept warm in the office and got on friendly terms with Frank again.

All this came to an end on my birthday on the 26th of April when the bombshell metaphorically dropped.

I was congratulating myself on having reached the ripe old age of twenty-three and still being in one piece after all my travels and tribulations, when a WAAF came into the office with a signal (a message on a slip of paper) which had just been received in the orderly room.

I had been transferred into the Army.

Not the ordinary Army but the PBI (Poor Bloody Infantry). It came as a bit of a shock to say the least but I now knew what the NCO's course at Filey had been about.

First, I had to go for a medical. Frank kept telling me to tell the medical officer that I had suffered with bad headaches ever since I had been in Iraq. Frank didn't seem to know about my nightmares so I didn't tell him. I did tell the medical officer but he didn't seem interested and passed me 'A1'.

After another day or two a message came through that I had to report to RAF Weeton near Blackpool on May third.

When I arrived at Weeton there were lots of lads from the RAF Regiment who were also being transferred into the infantry. There were also some observers like myself but none from my old unit.

On my first morning at Weeton, whilst I was in the ablutions getting washed, an airman came bursting in. He was so excited that at first I couldn't tell what he was going on about. When he settled down a bit he said it had just been announced on the eight o'clock news that the Germans had packed it in.

The next day was Victory in Europe day and that was the day I got discharged from the RAF and more or less press-ganged into the Army.

That night I went into Blackpool. Everyone was in the streets and on the sea front celebrating. I had a few pints and went to the Tower Ballroom. They had to close the Ballroom early as some revellers were letting off fireworks that caused a big fire risk.

I walked a nurse back to the hospital at Poulton-le-Fylde and made my way back to camp.

It was a long walk to Weeton, which gave me time to think about the good times and the bad times of the last five years. Summing it all up I came to the conclusion that in five years they had changed me from a naïve youth into a cynical, broken hearted, petty thief and murderer.

The next day I was on my way to Northern Ireland to start all over again.